LIFE AND DEATH OF CHARLOTTE SALOMON

PETER SCHUMANN

This book was collectively designed around a kitchen table by Donna Bister, Marc Estrin, Elka & Peter Schumann

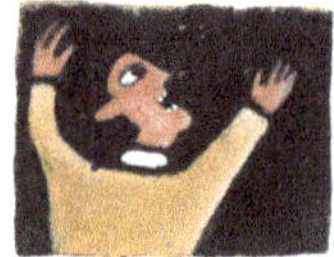

ISBN 978-1-944388-32-4
Library of Congress Number 2018944755

06/06/2026

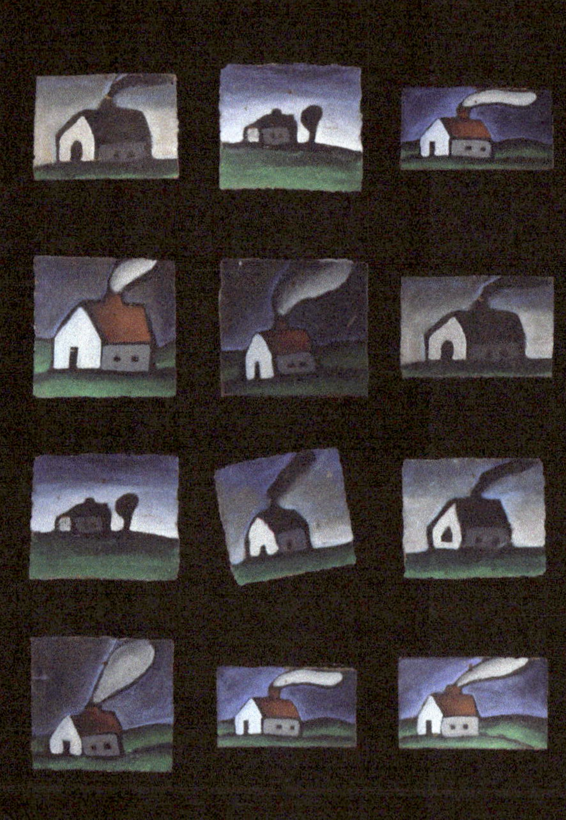

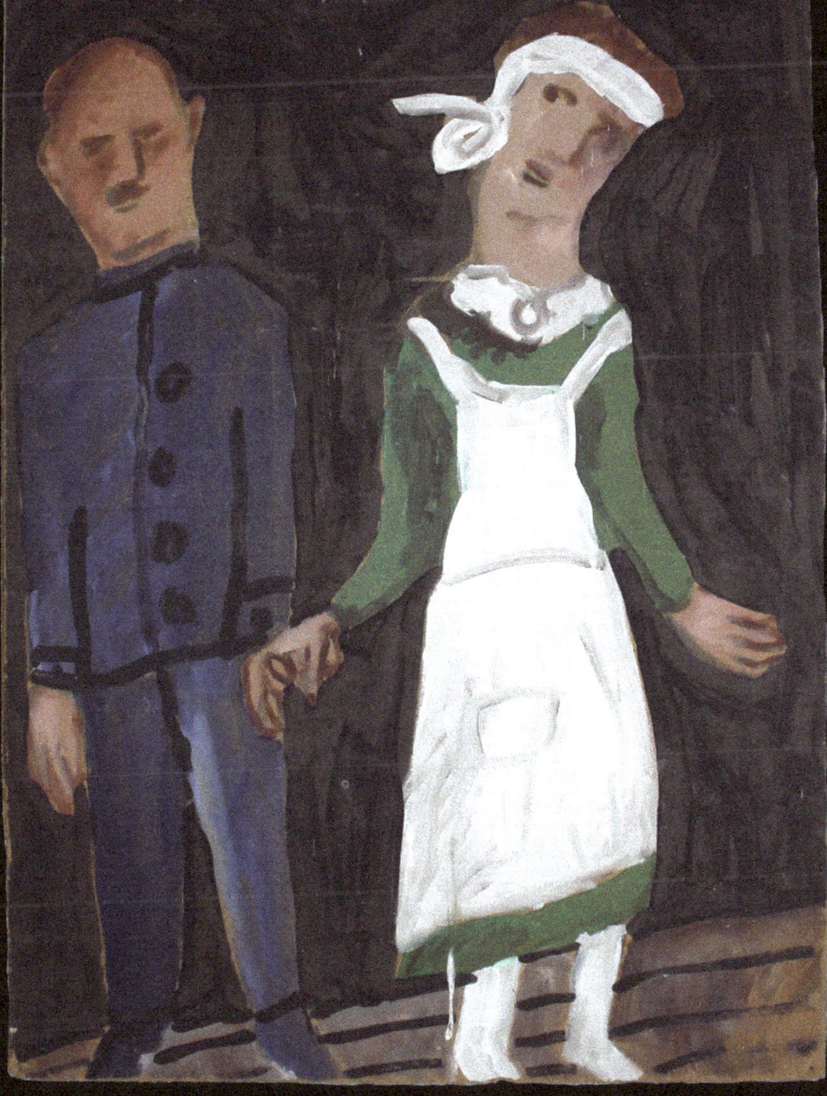
CHARLOTTE'S MOTHER, FRANZISKA, WHO WAS A
VOLUNTEER NURSE IN THE FIRST WORLD WAR
PRESENTS HER FIANCE, A SURGEON WHOM
SHE MET IN A MILITARY HOSPITAL
TO HER PARENTS

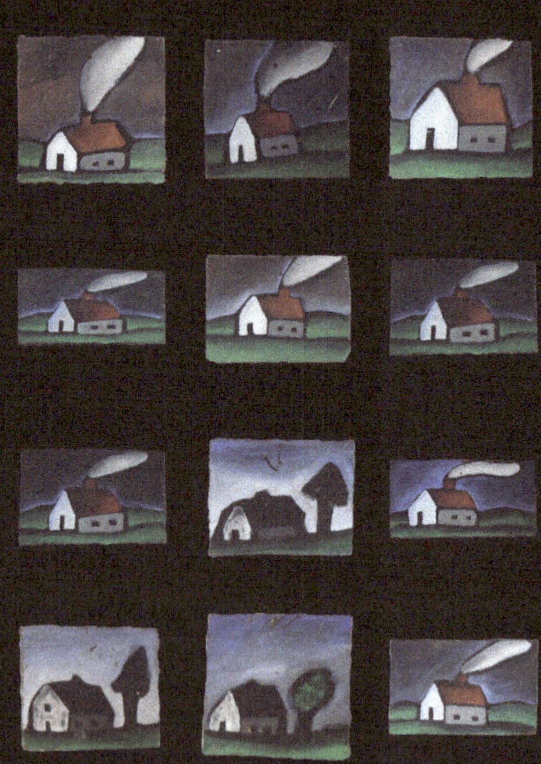

THE REGISTRAR OF THE GERMAN EMPIRE PLACES THE RING ON THE FINGER OF THE HAPPY BRIDE

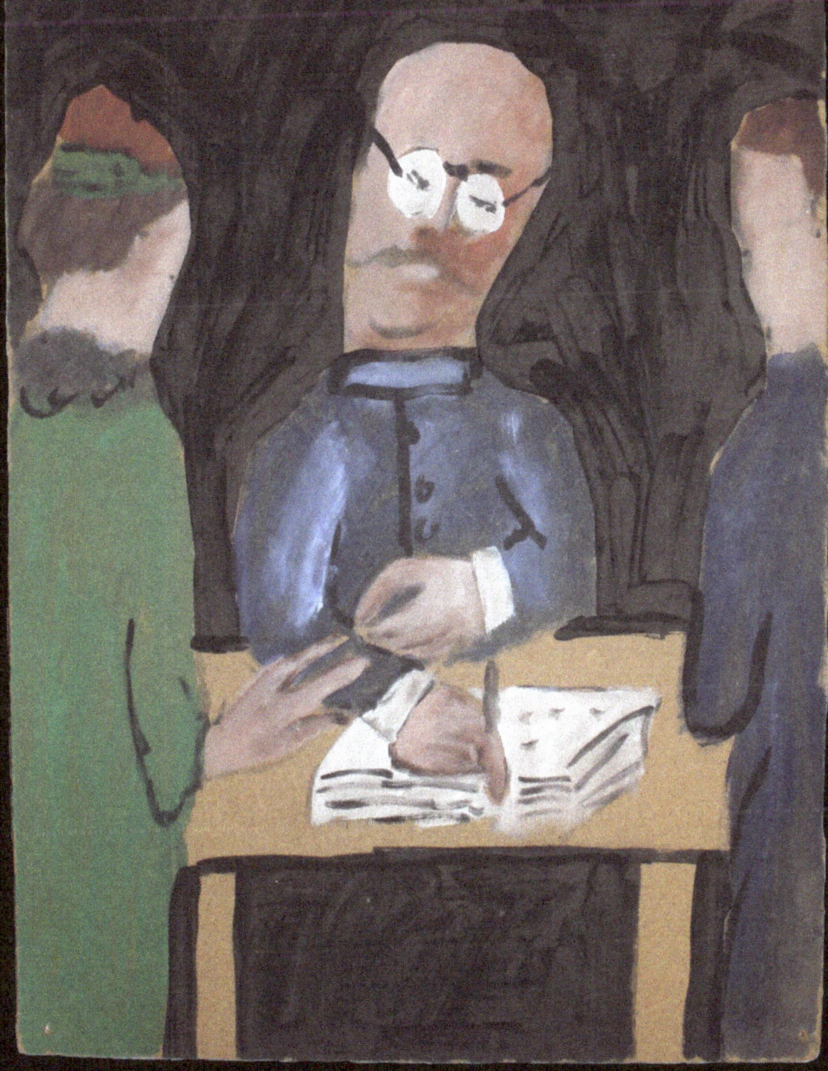

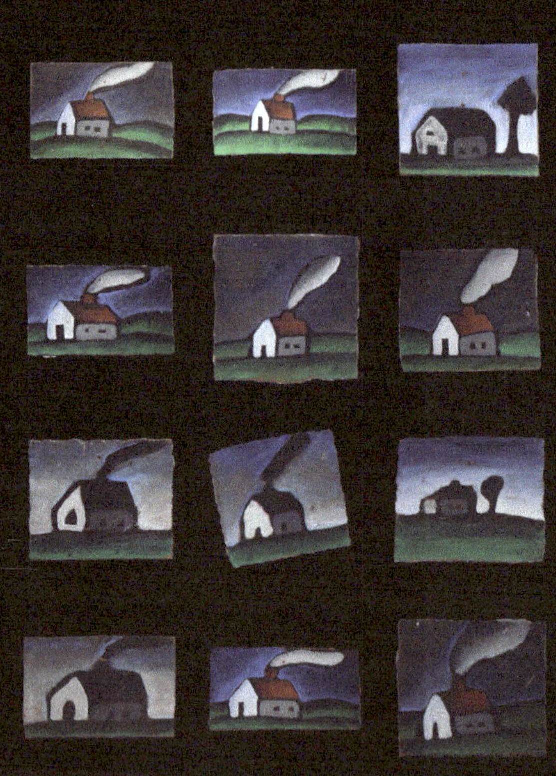

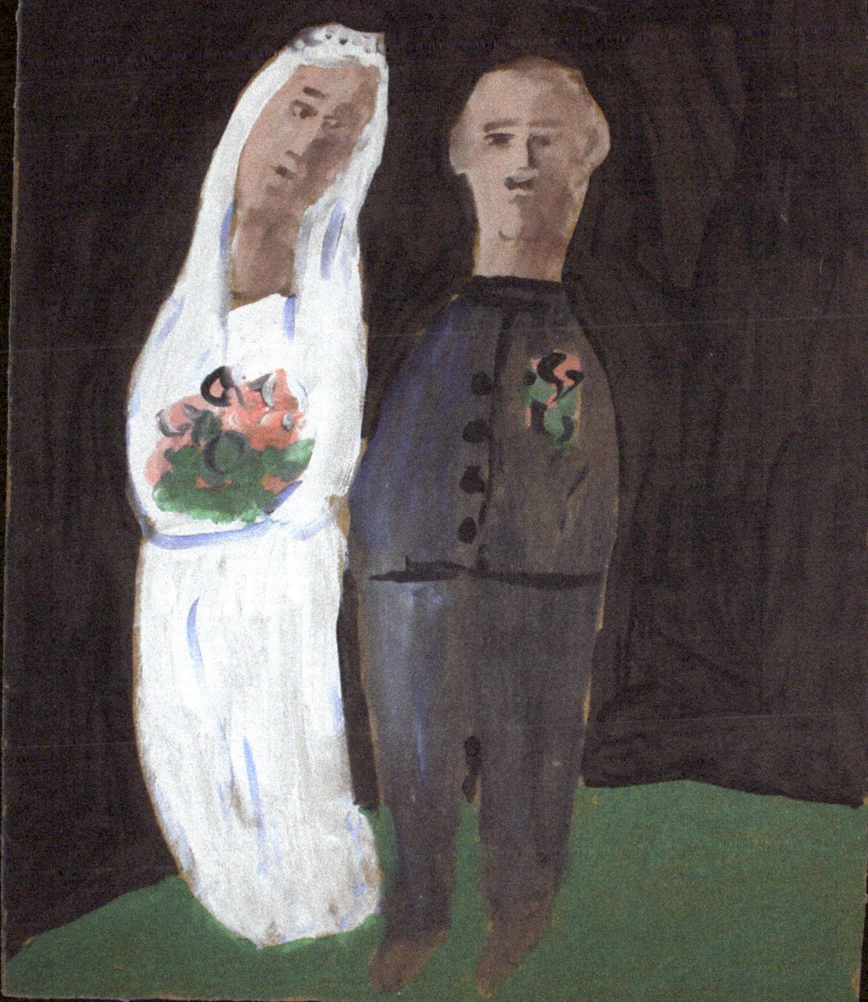
SHE IS RADIANT

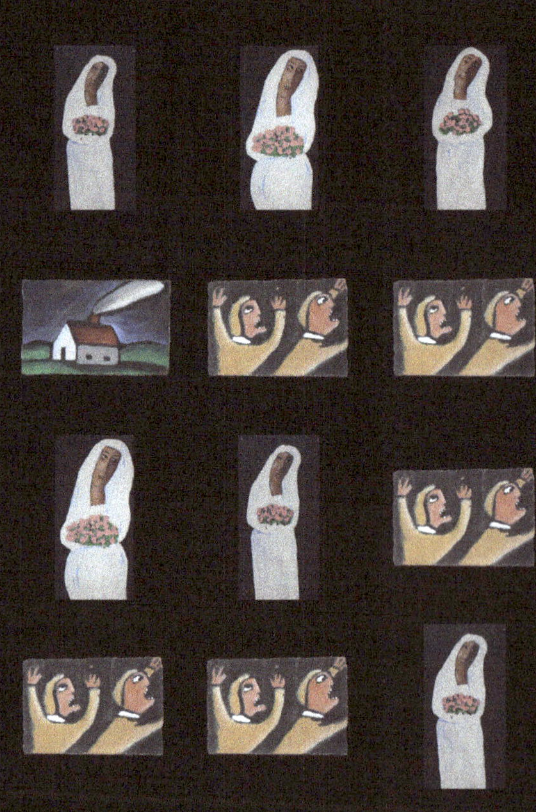

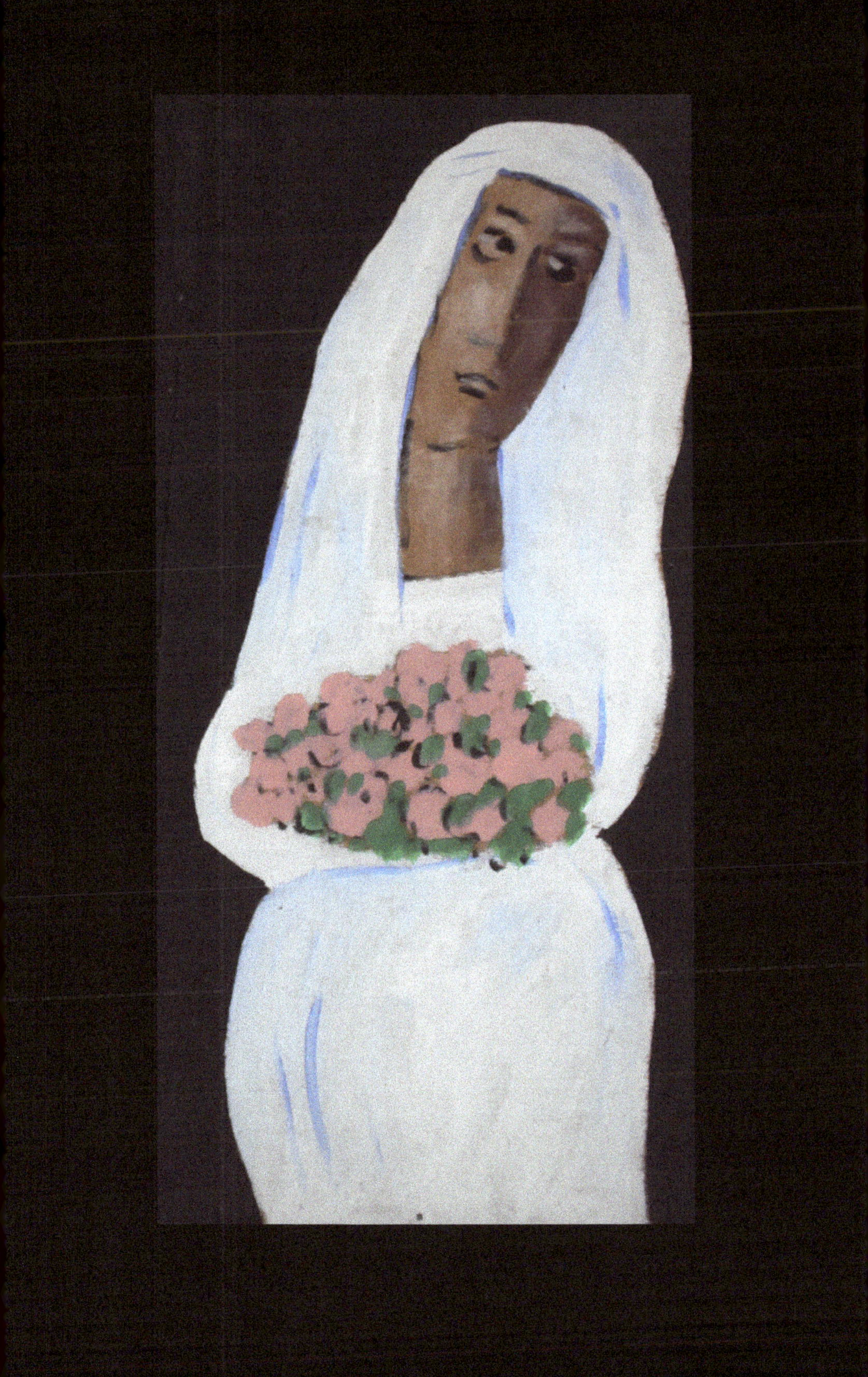

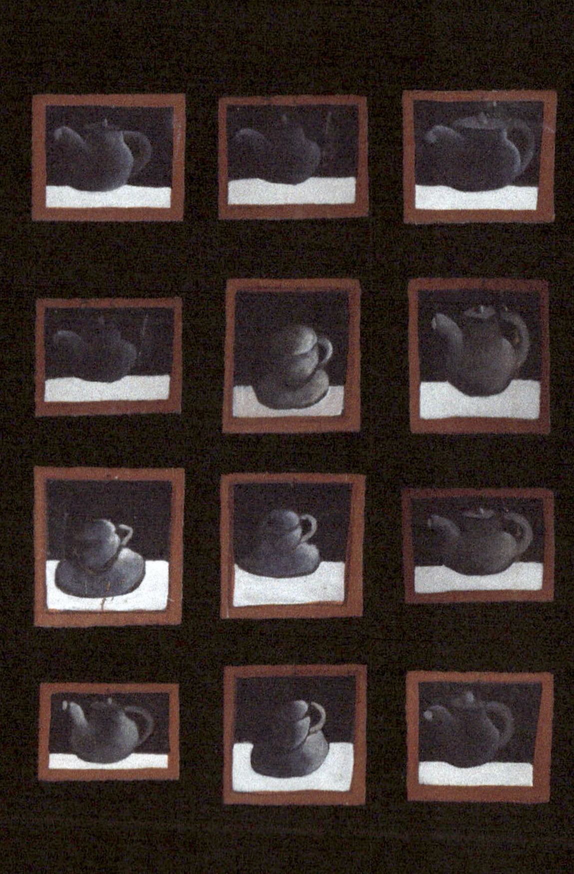

BARELY A YEAR LATER, THE WAR WAS AT AN END.
FRANZISKA'S HUSBAND ALBERT RETURNED SHORTLY BEFORE THE BIRTH OF THEIR FIRST CHILD: CHARLOTTE

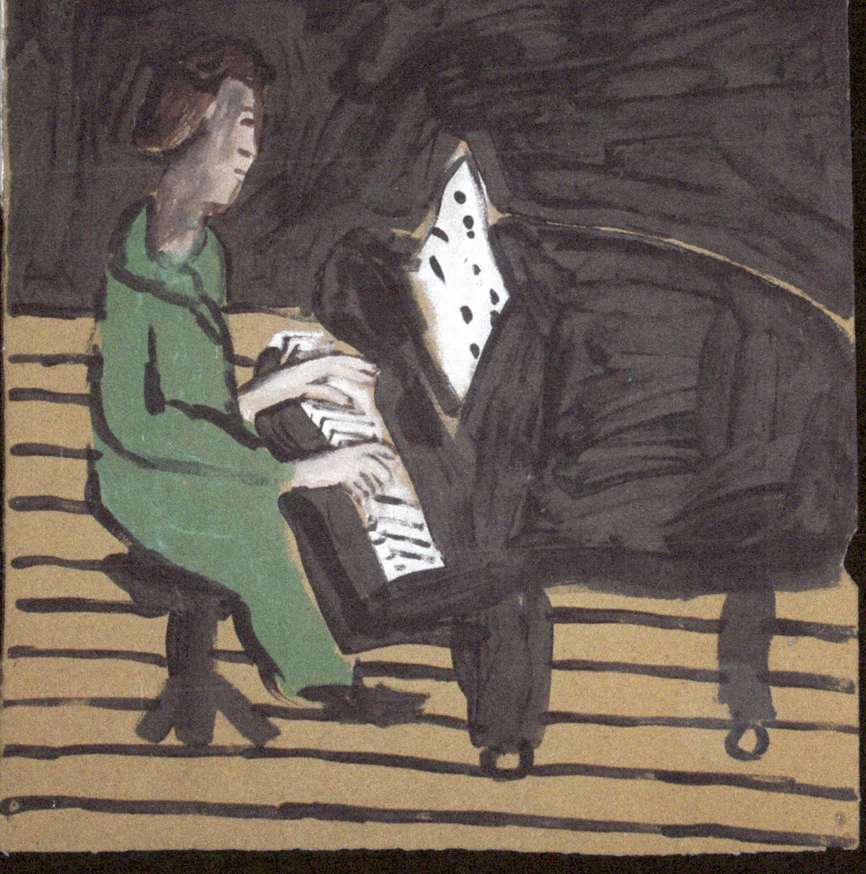

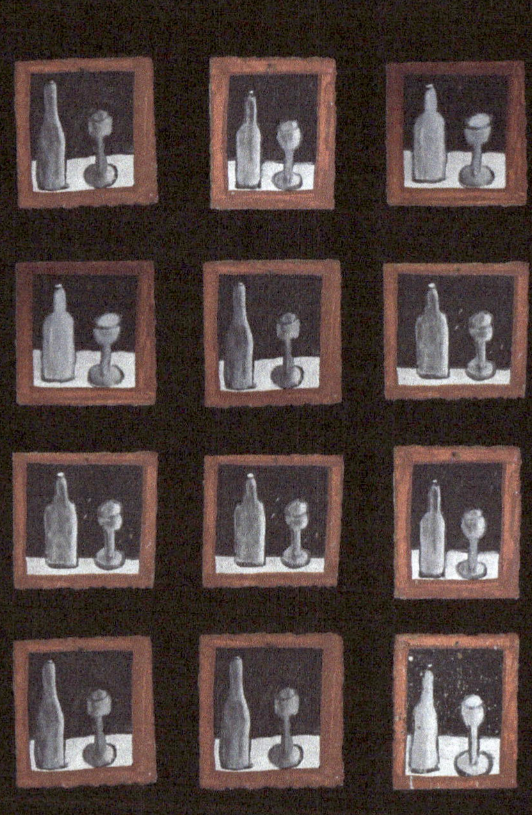

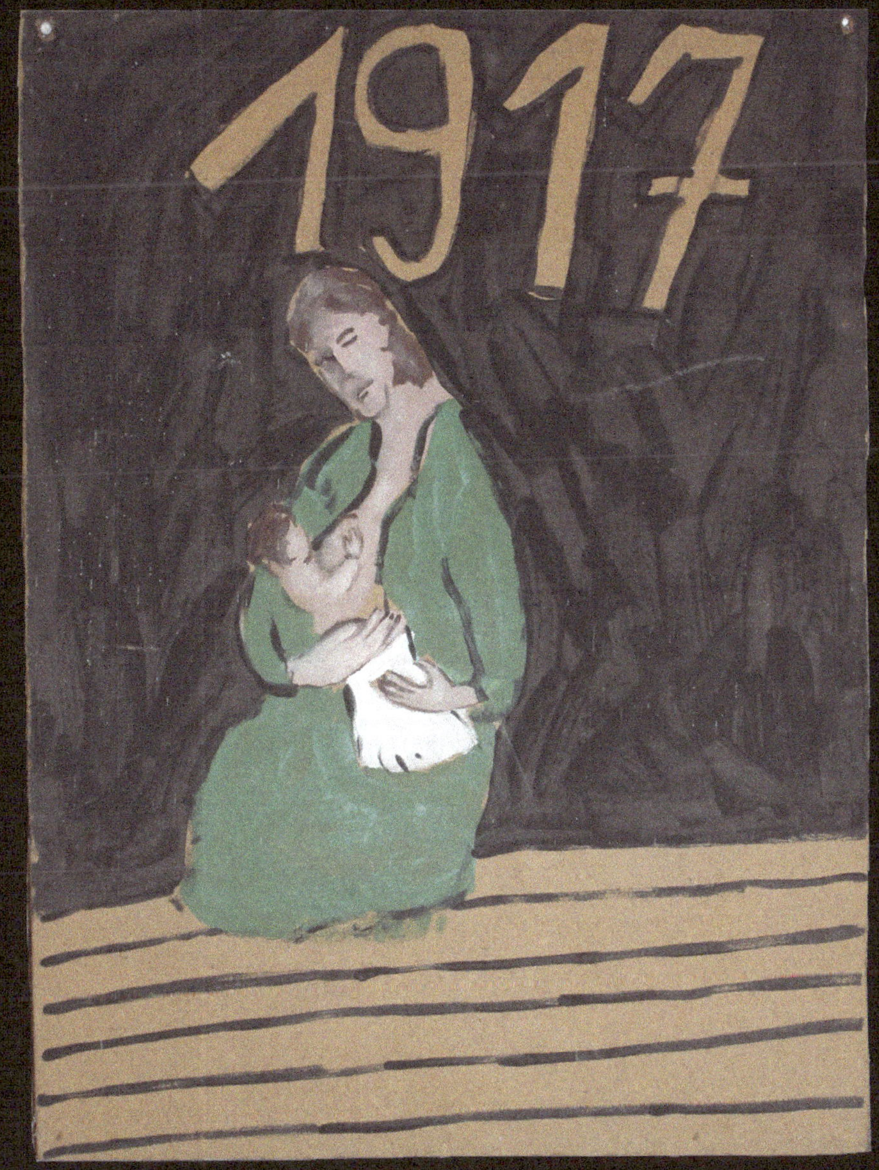
1917

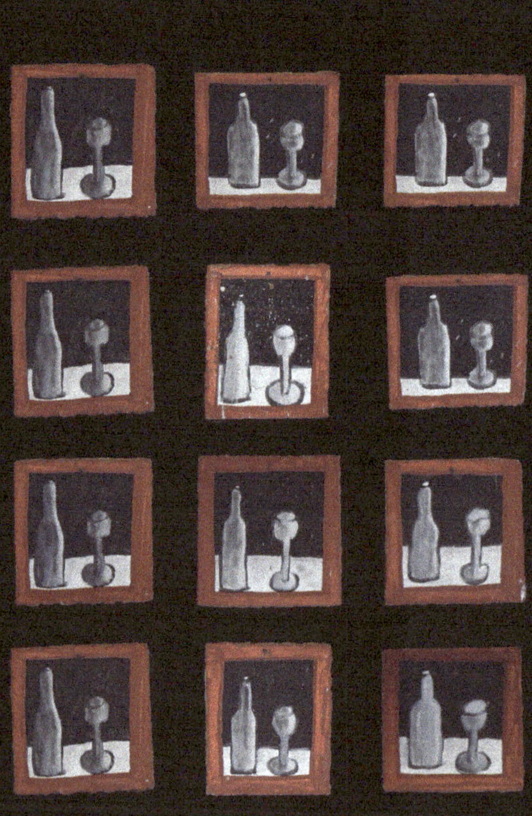

SHE INSISTED ON PUSHING THE TALL WHITE BABY CARRIAGE

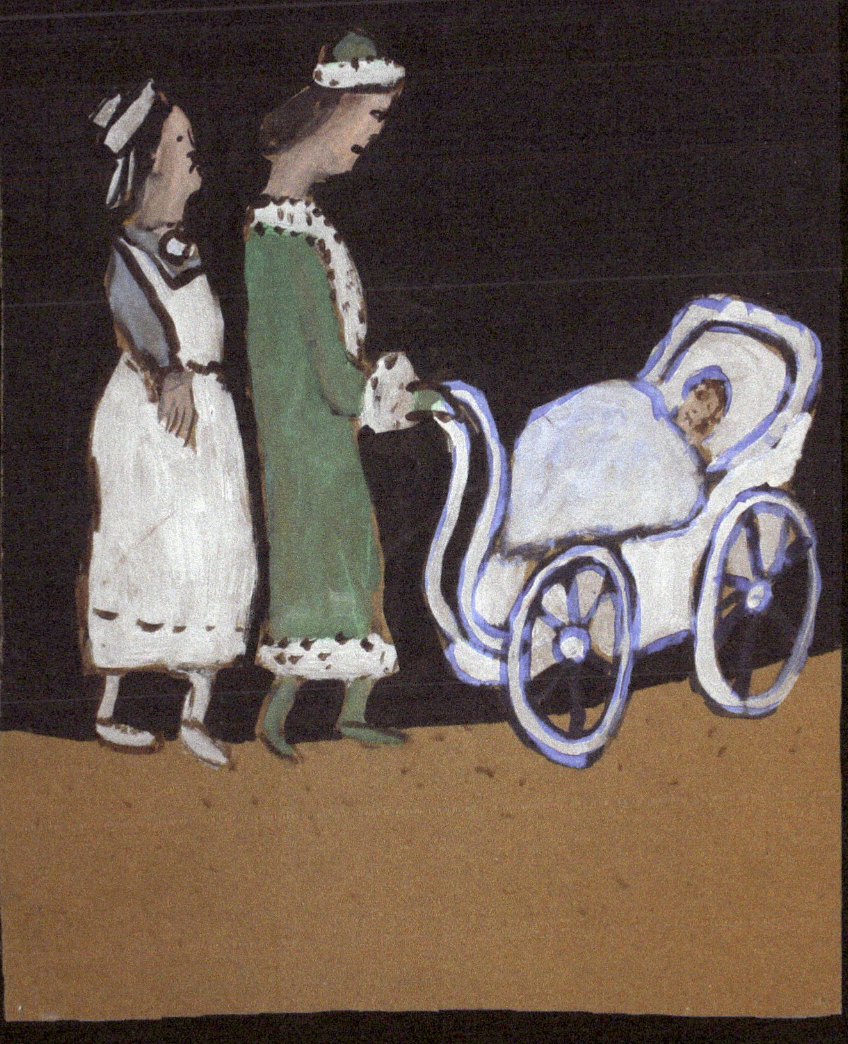

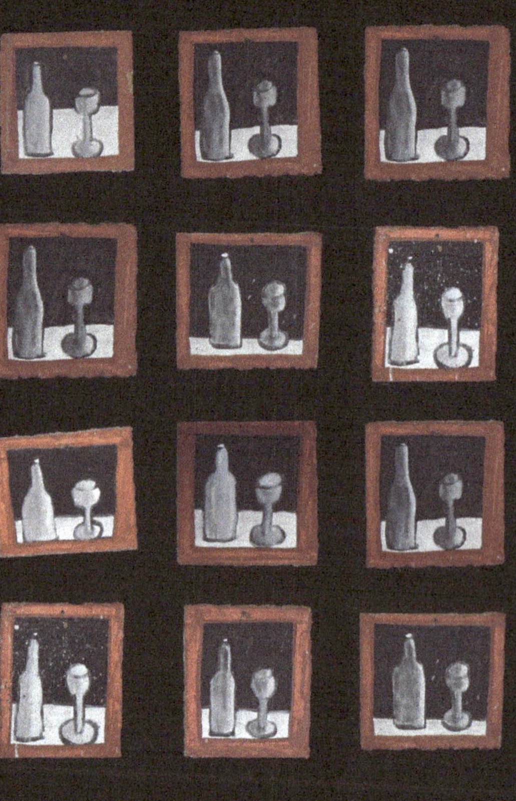

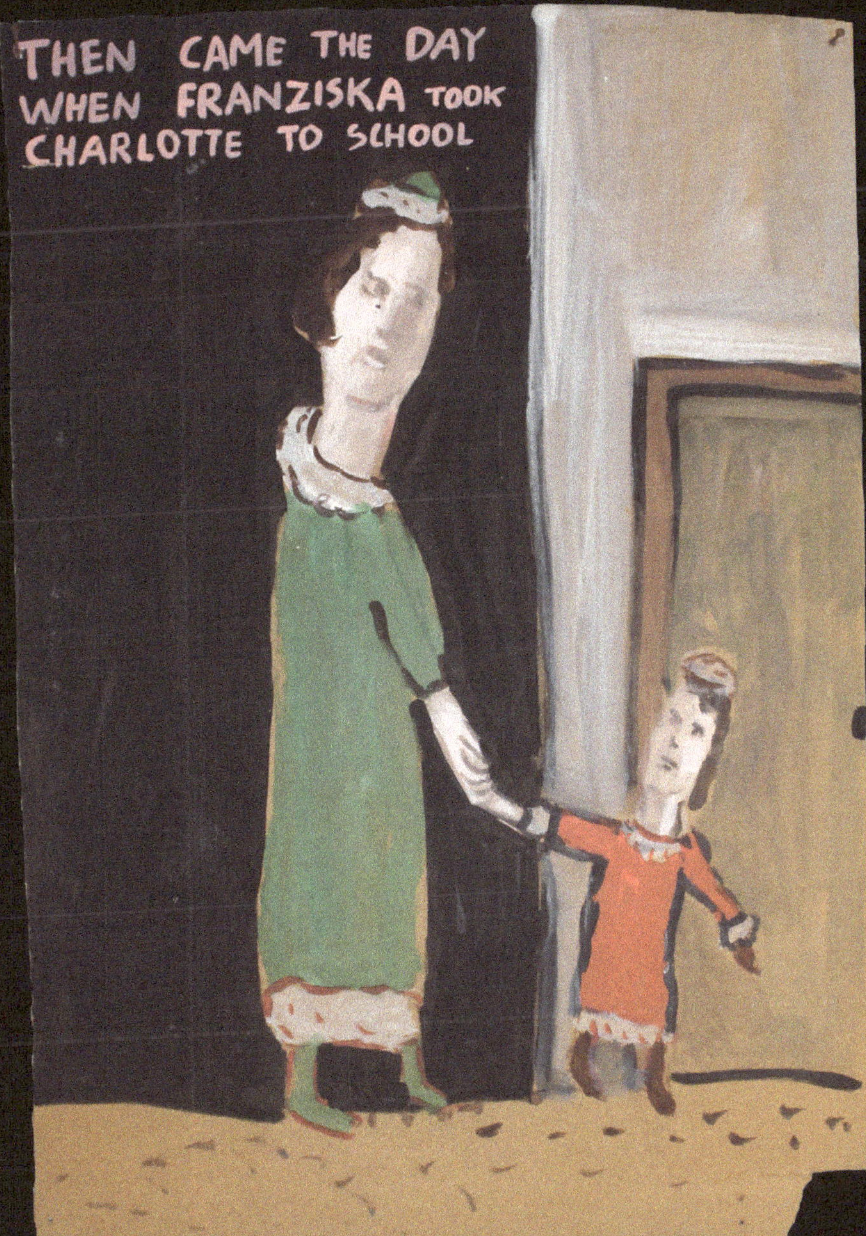
THEN CAME THE DAY
WHEN FRANZISKA TOOK
CHARLOTTE TO SCHOOL

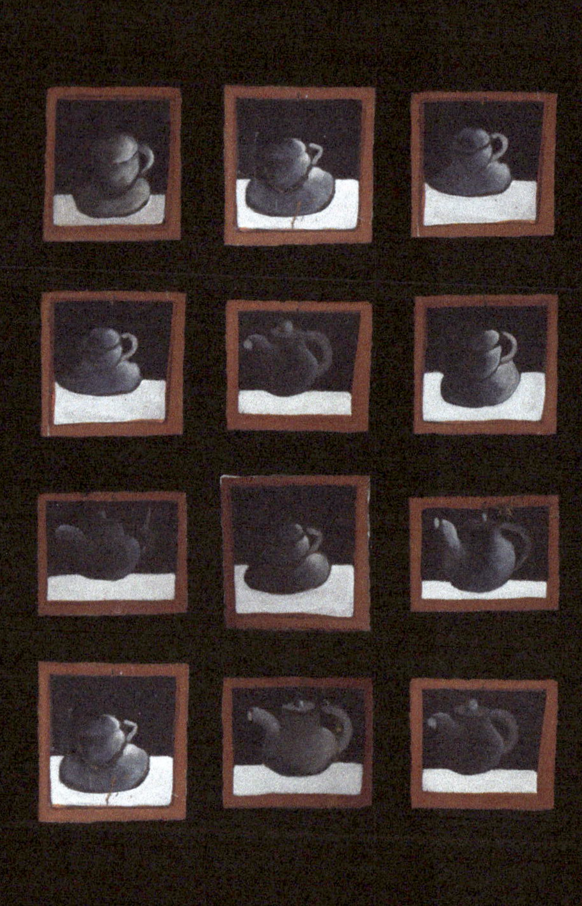

CHARLOTTE'S MOTHER WAS HIGHLY EMOTIONAL. OFTEN SHE TOOK THE CHILD TO BED WITH HER AND TOLD HER STORIES ABOUT LIFE AFTER DEATH IN HEAVEN

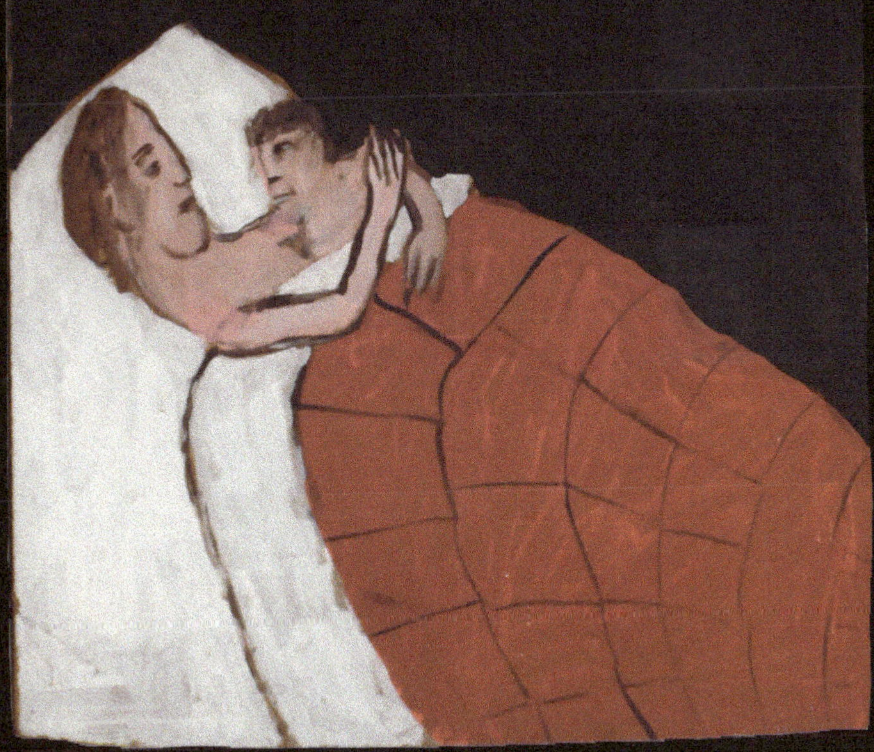

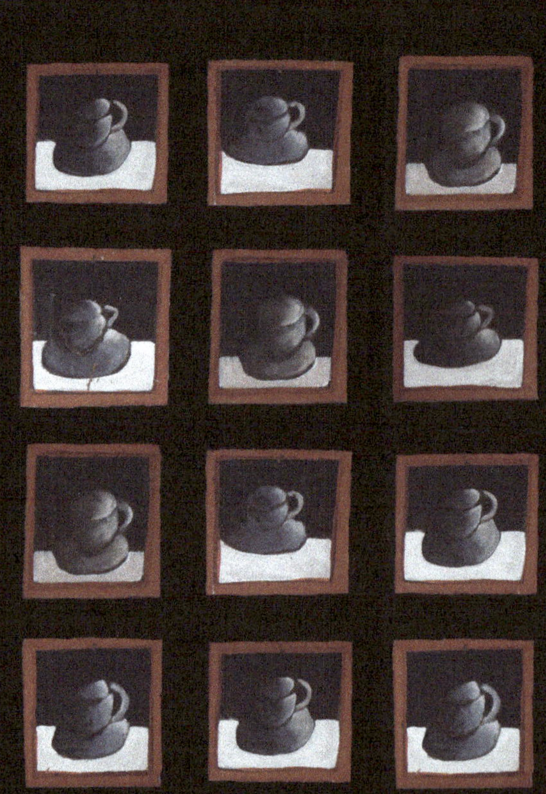

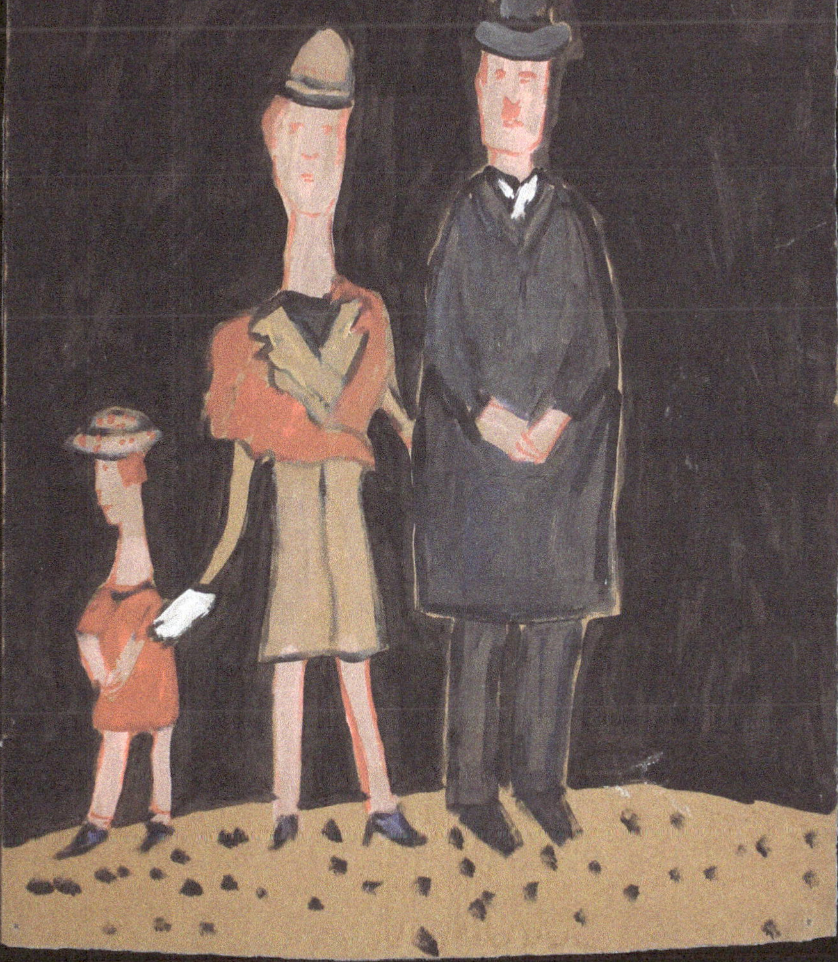
THEN, ALL OF A SUDDEN, CHARLOTTE'S MOTHER CEASED TO TAKE PLEASURE IN ANYTHING. ALL SHE TALKED OF WAS DYING

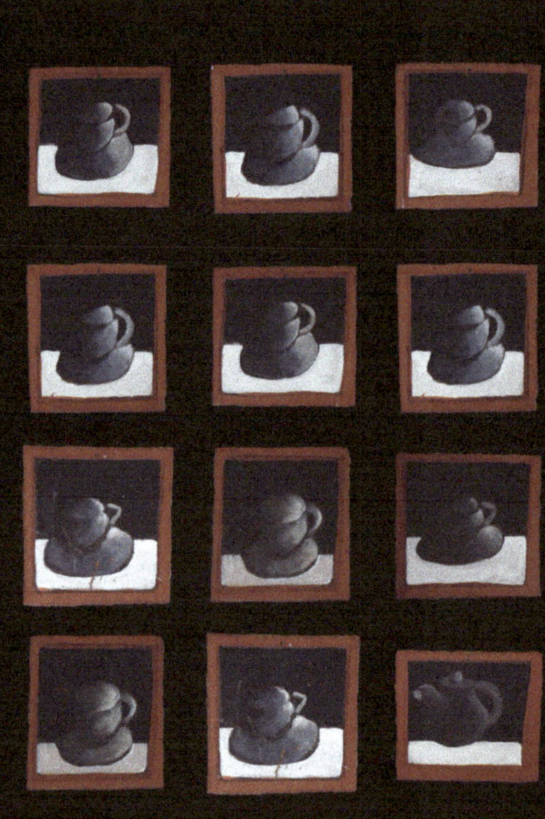

HER HUSBAND PLEADED
WITH HER. BUT IT DIDN'T
HELP

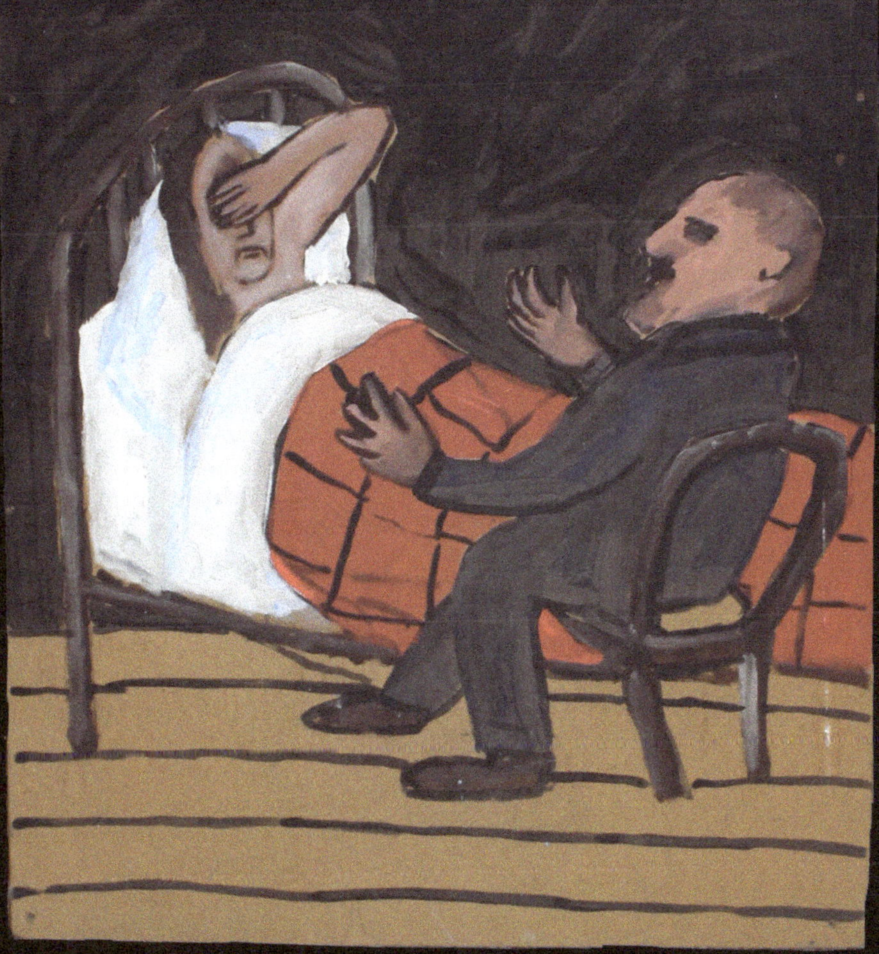

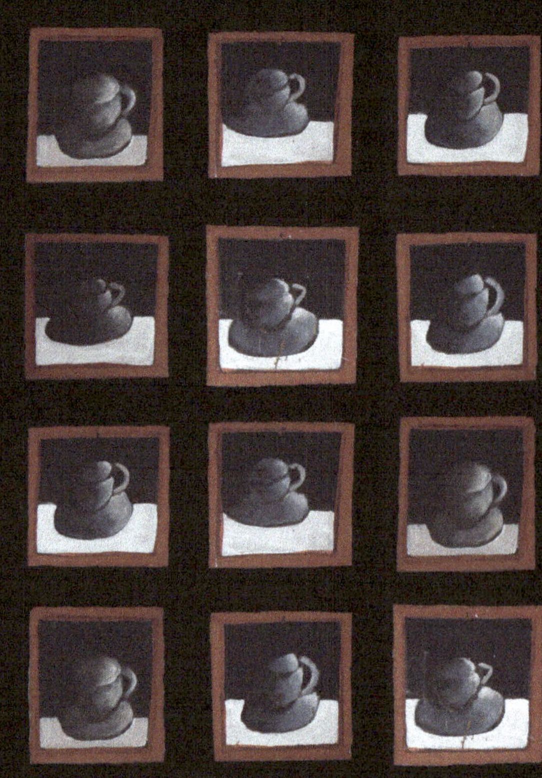

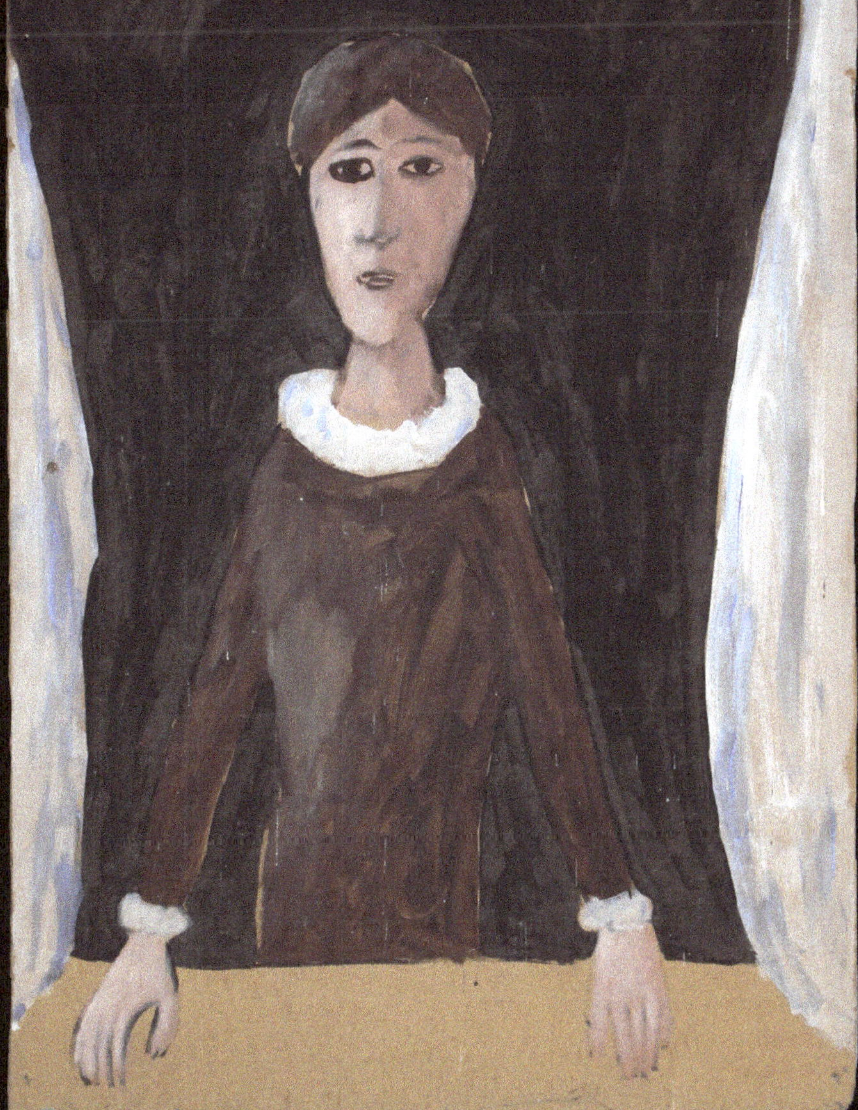
FOR A LONG TIME SHE
STOOD AT THE WINDOW

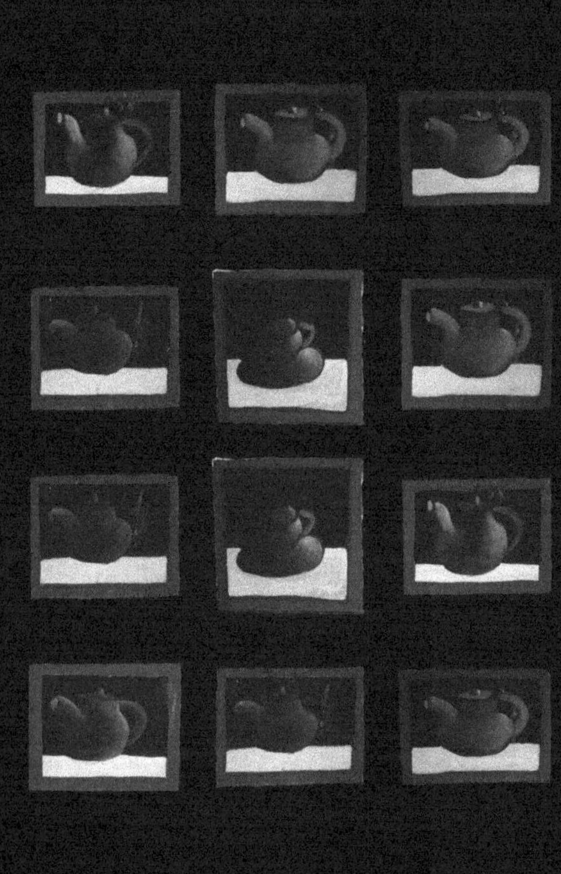

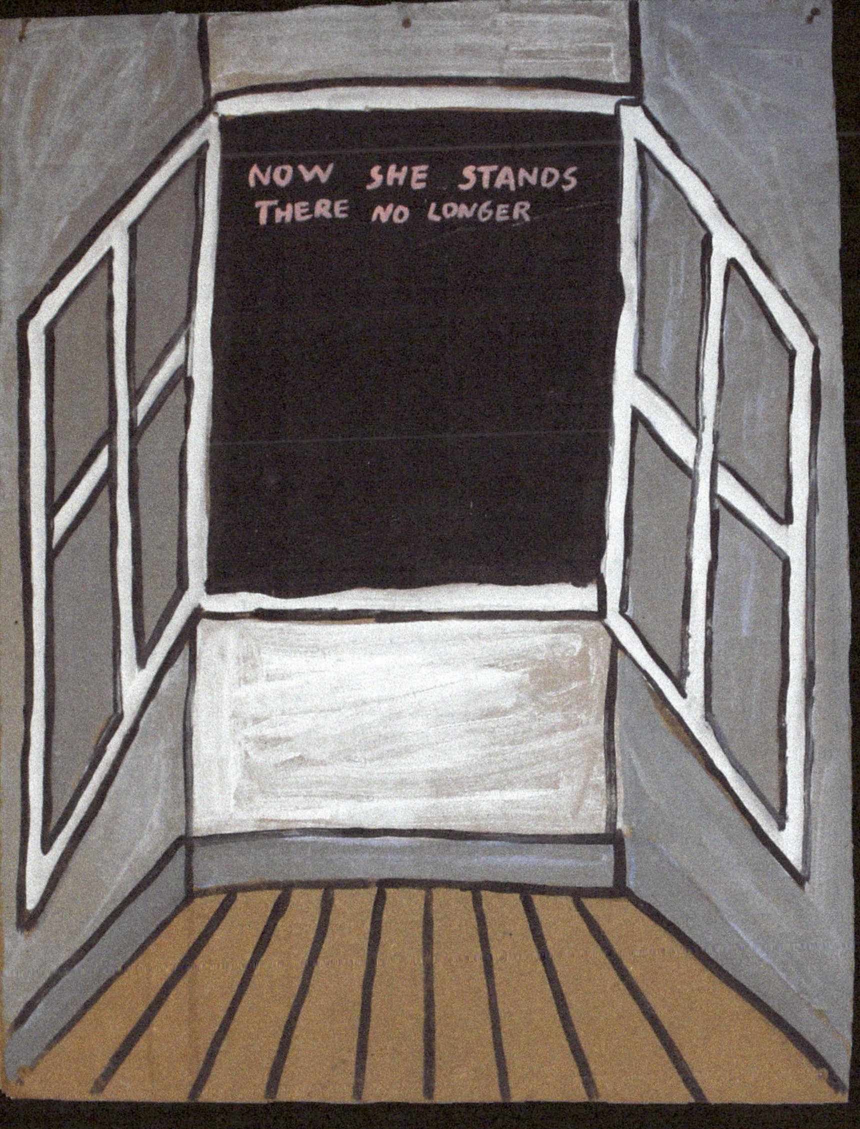
NOW SHE STANDS
THERE NO LONGER

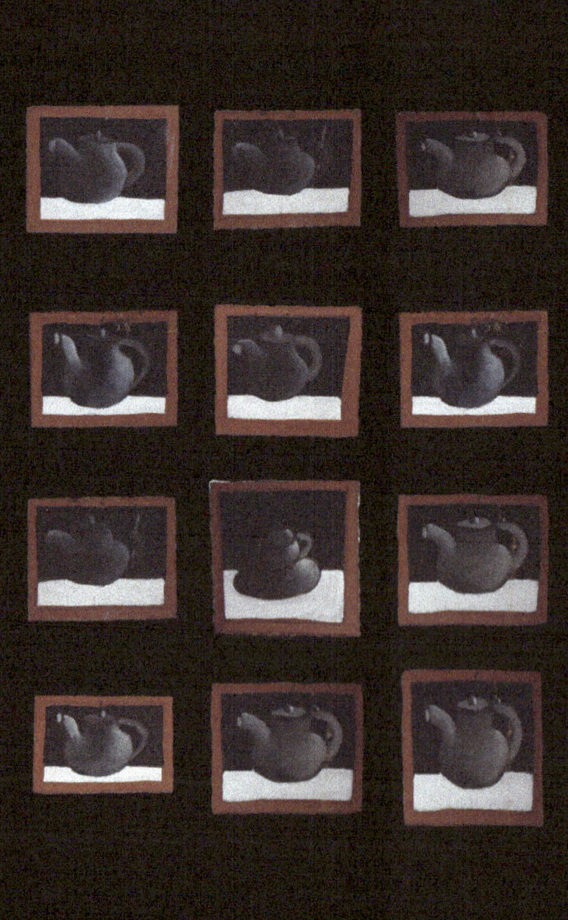

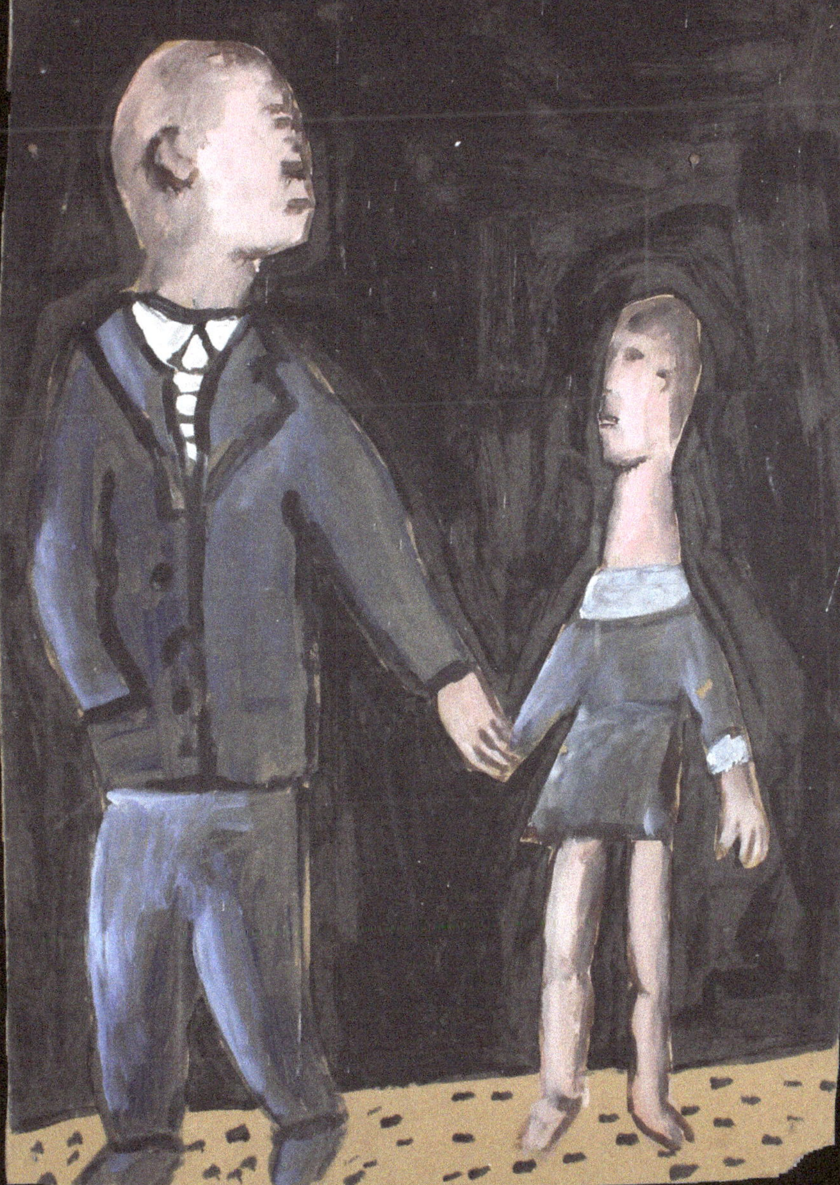
ALAS, WE HAVE LOST HER

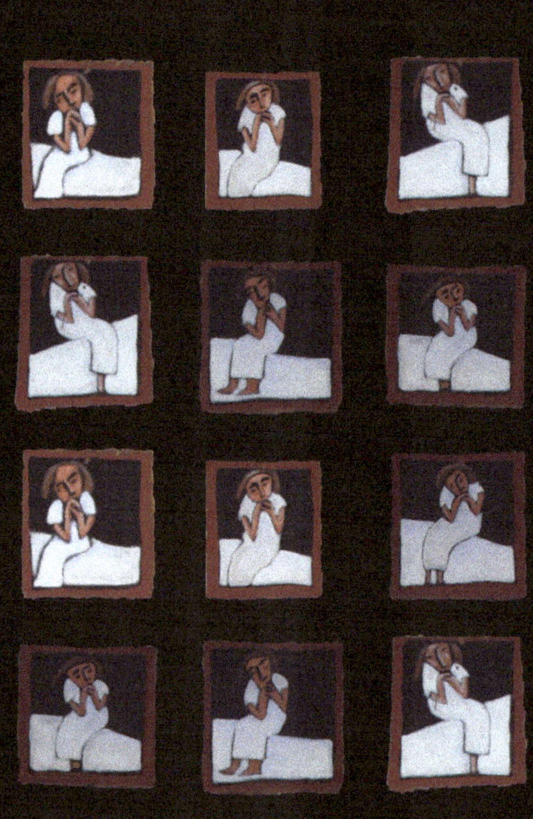

JANUARY 30, 1933

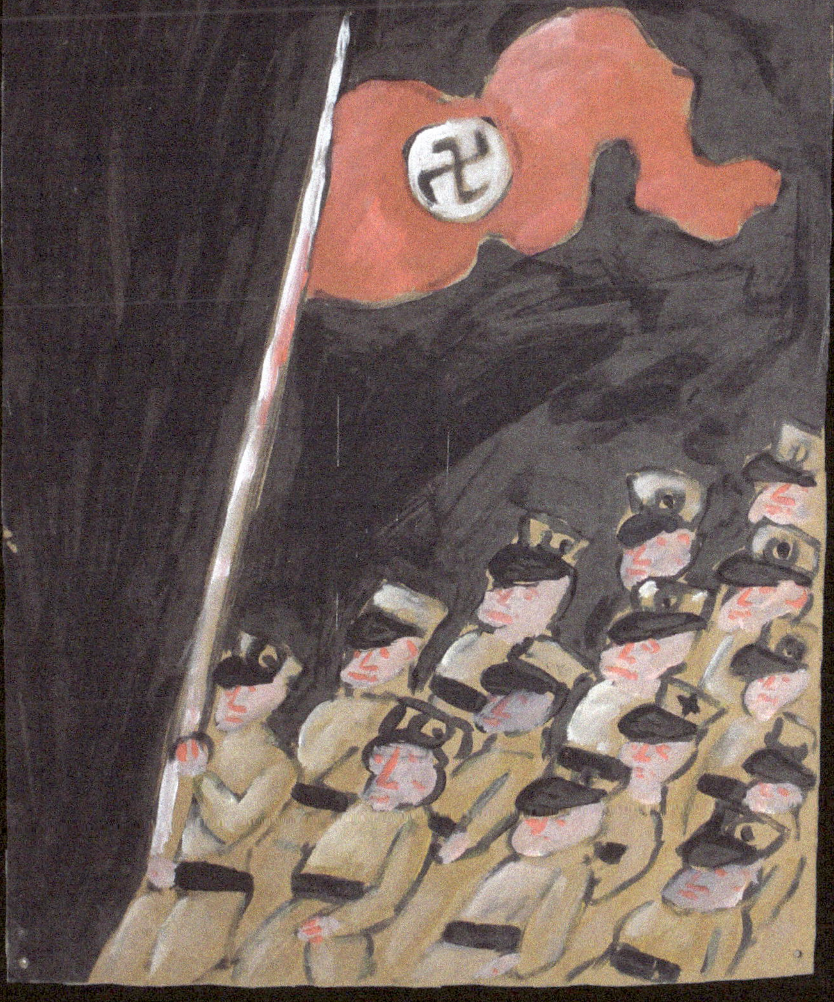

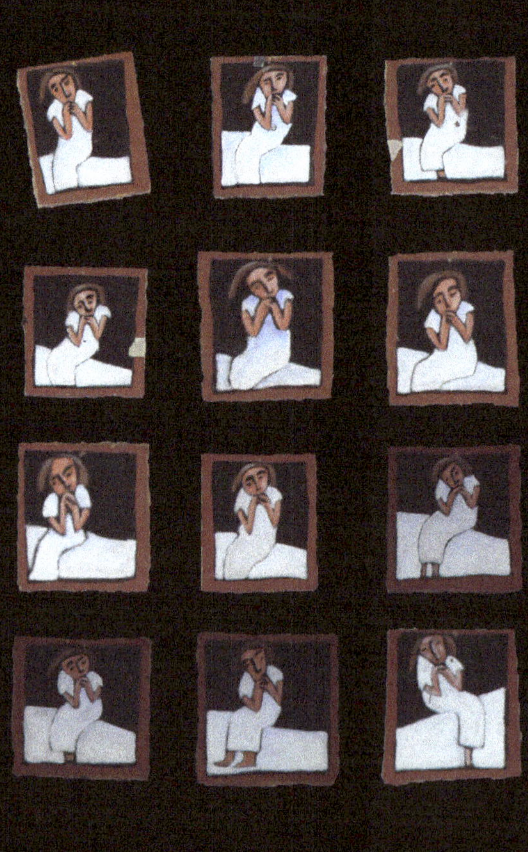

THE SWASTIKA MAKES ITS APPEARANCE IN THE SCHOOL ALSO.

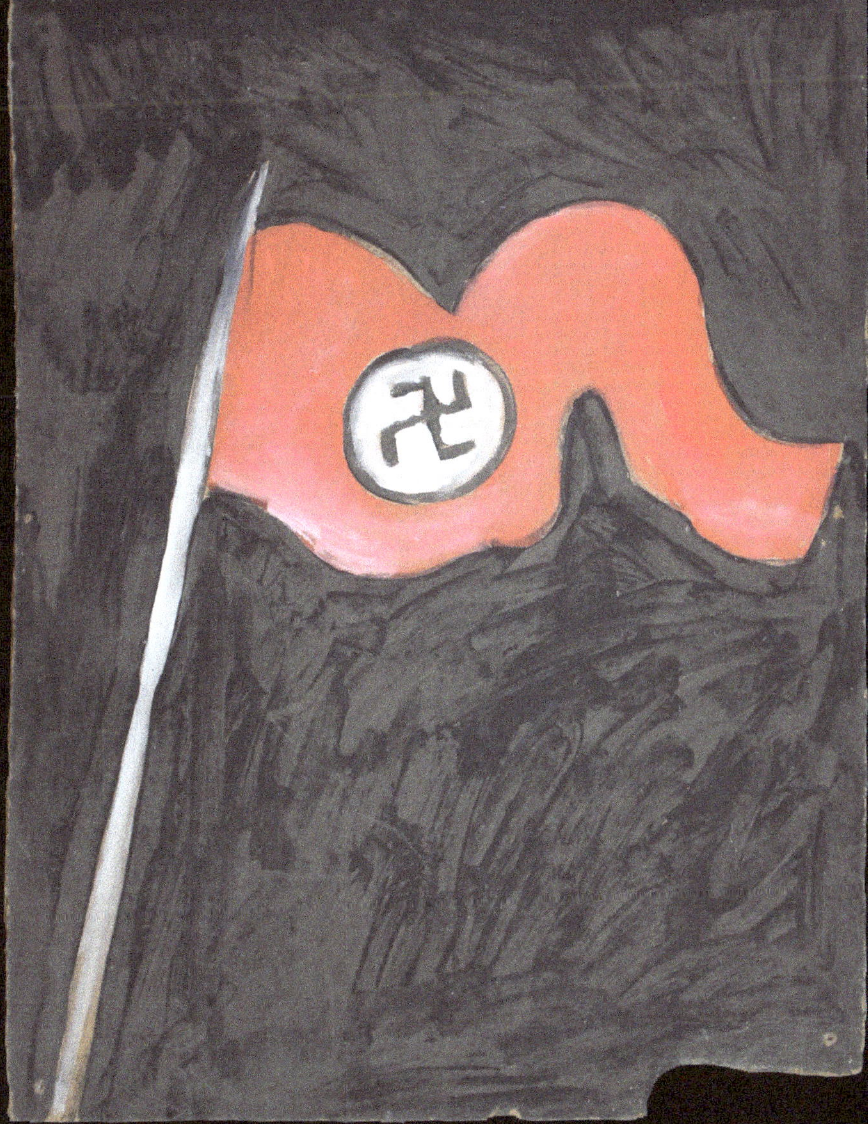

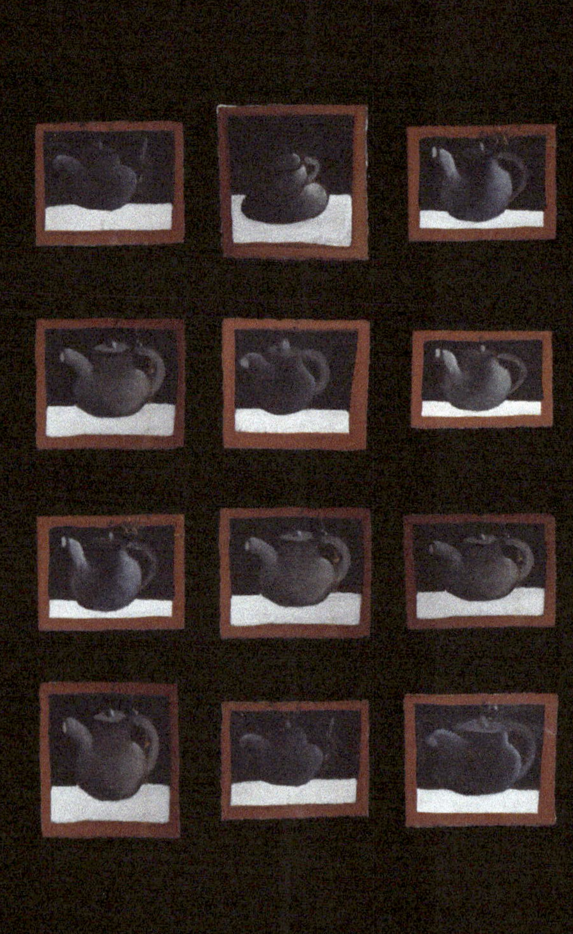

CHARLOTTE WAS DESPERATE. AT SCHOOL SHE WAS OFTEN SLAPPED. IT DISTRESSED HER FATHER, BUT THERE WAS NOTHING HE COULD DO ABOUT IT

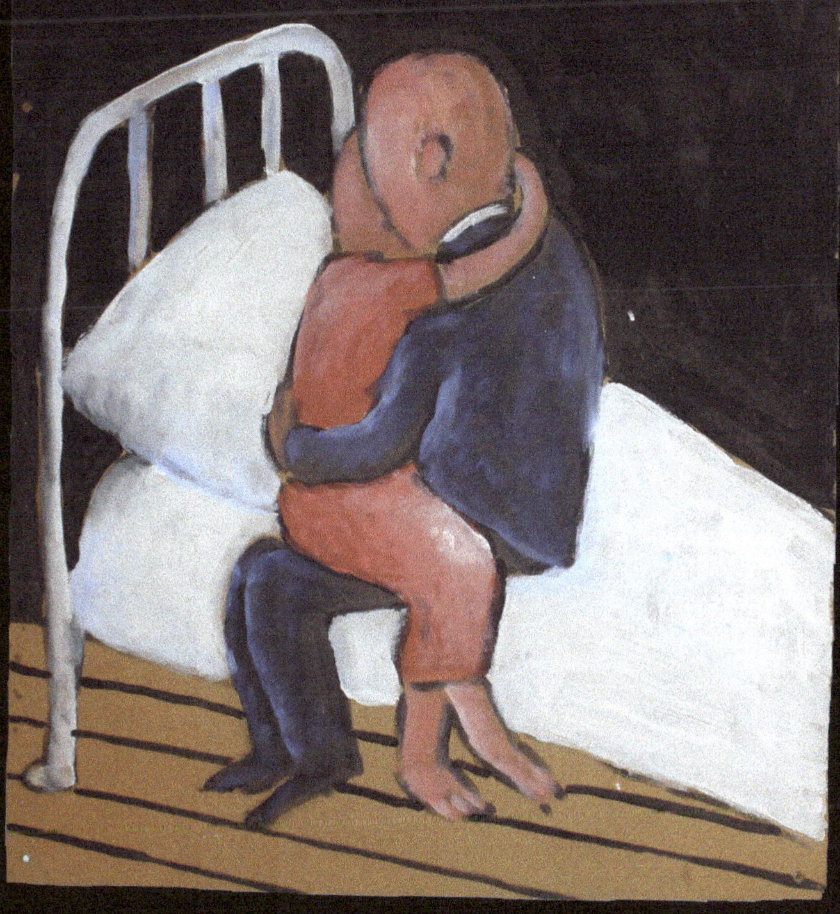

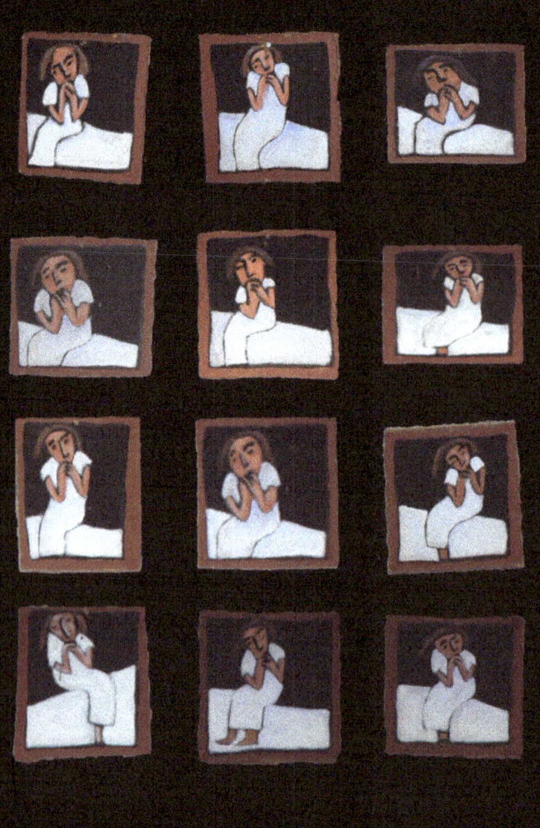

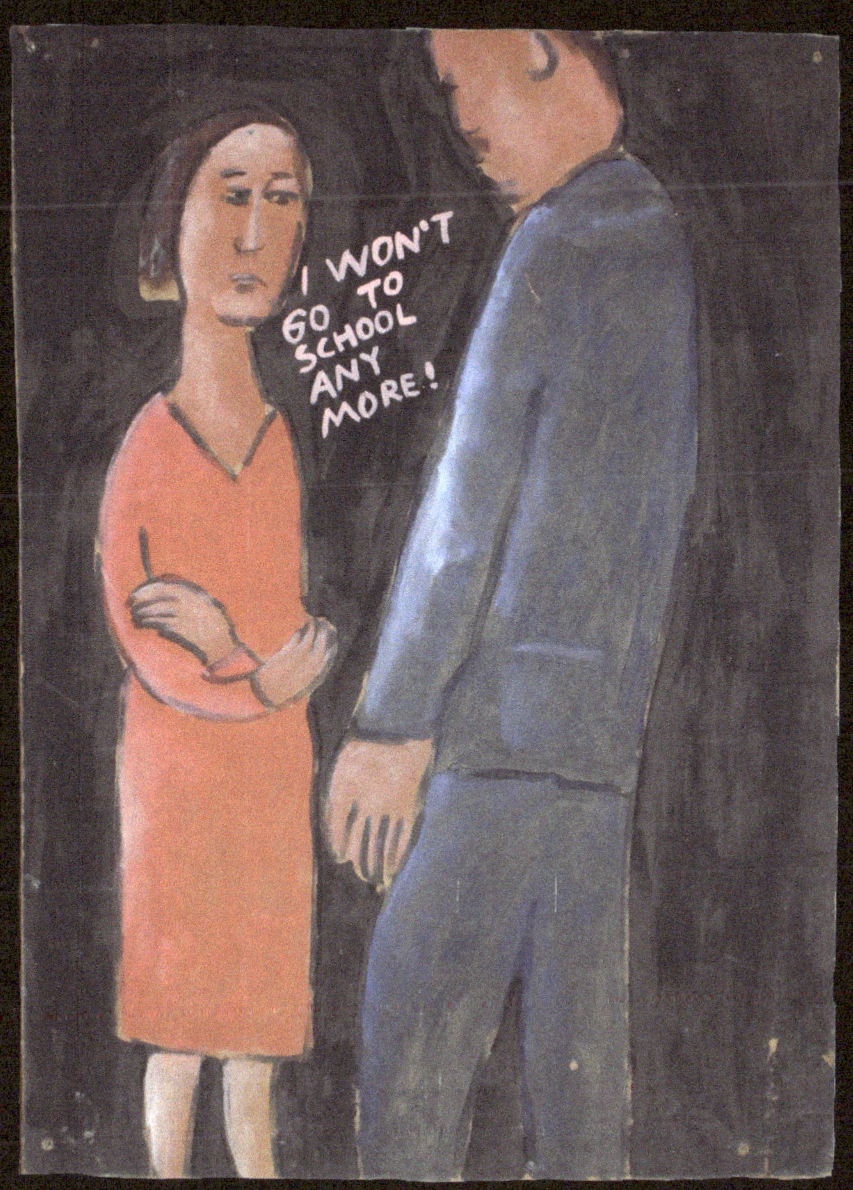
I WON'T GO TO SCHOOL ANY MORE!

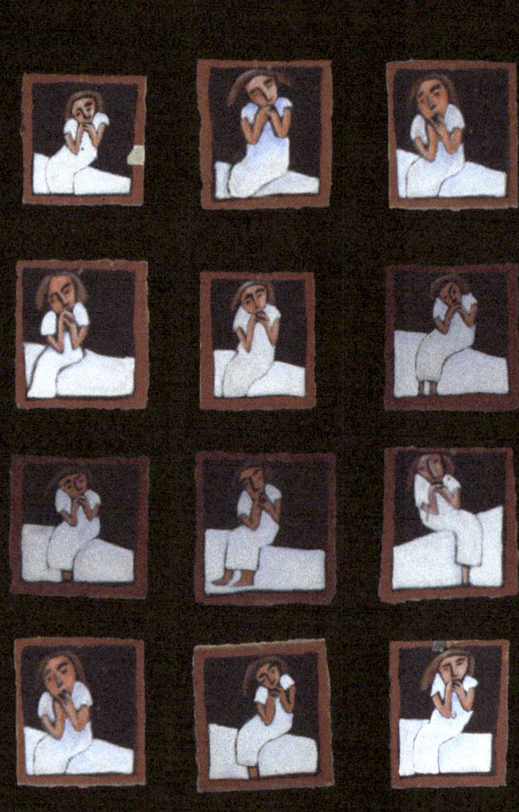

AFTER MANY DIFFICULTIES THE STATE ACADEMY OF FINE ARTS ACCEPTS CHARLOTTE AS A PUPIL ALTHOUGH SHE IS JEWISH

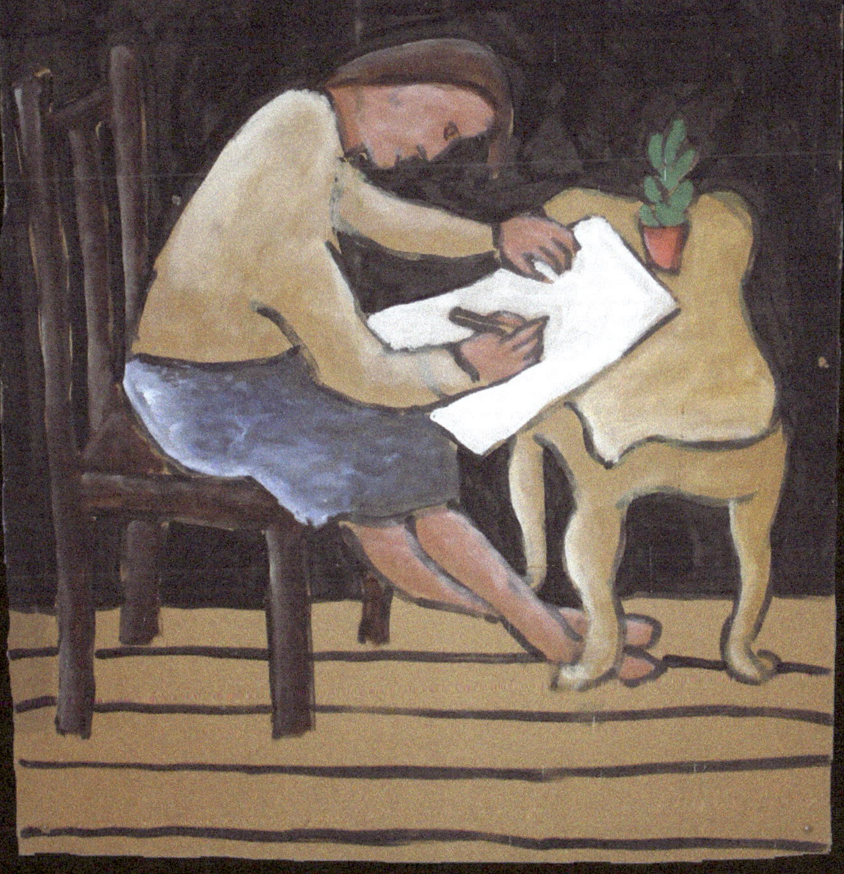

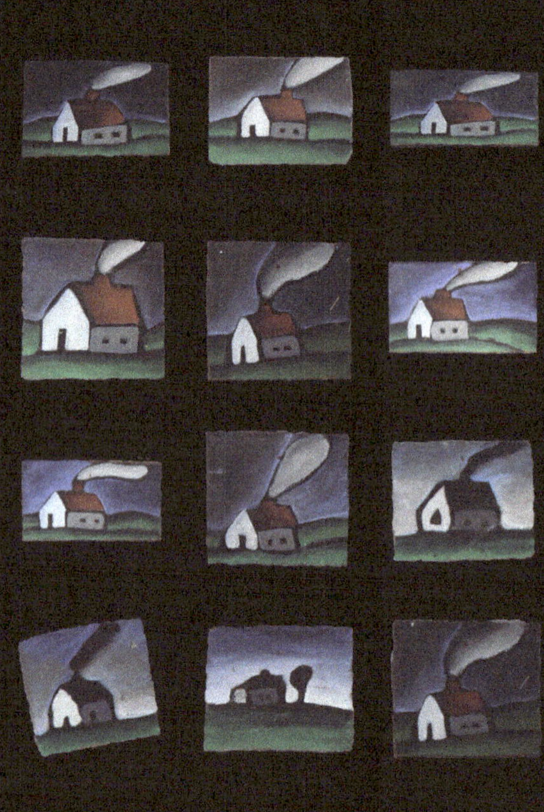

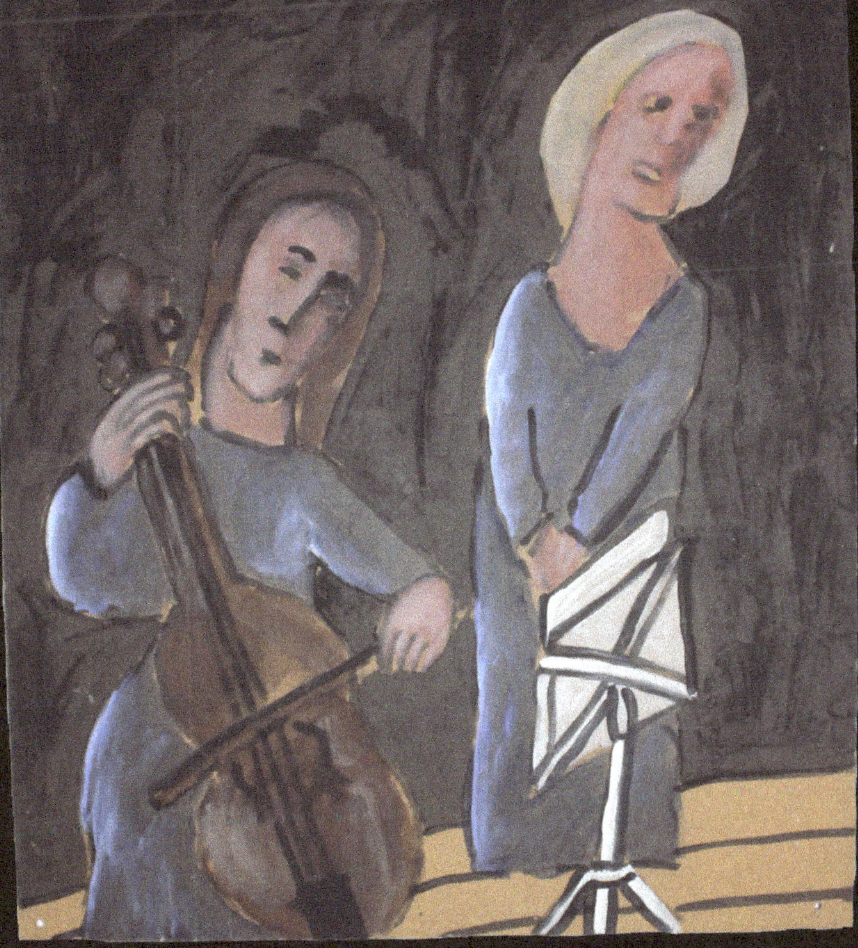
AT A PARTY THEY MEET A SINGER,
PAULINKA, WHO SINGS THE BACH ARIA:
"STRIKE, O STRIKE, AWAITED HOUR!"

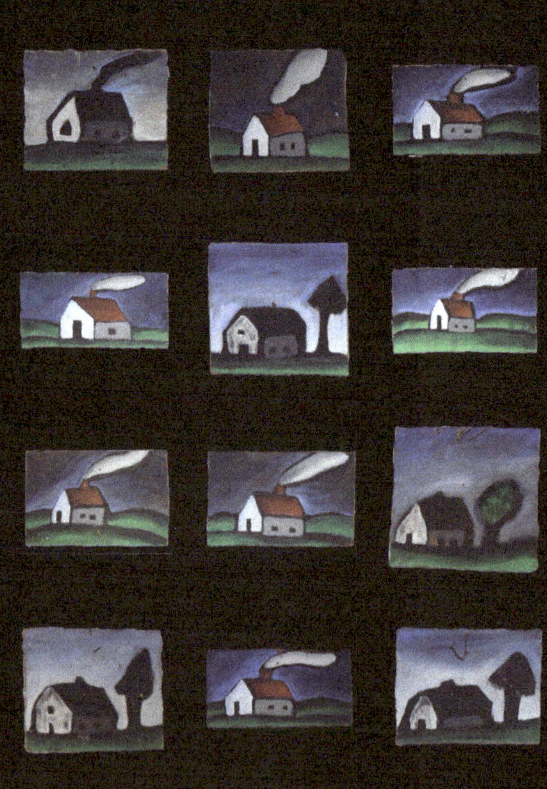

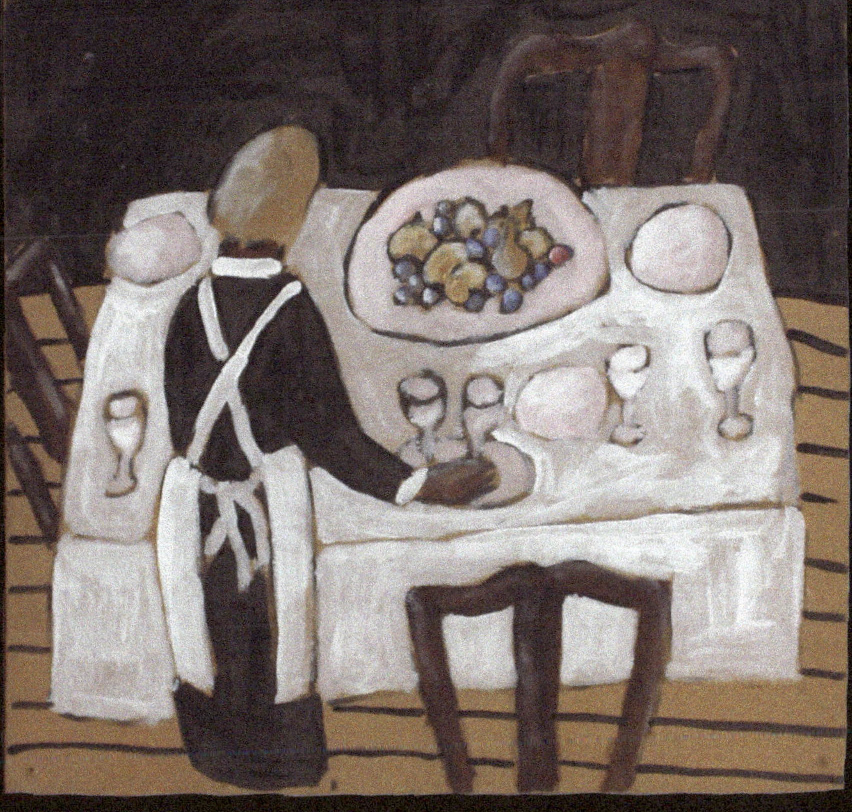
CHARLOTTE'S FATHER AND PAULINKA
DECIDED TO MARRY

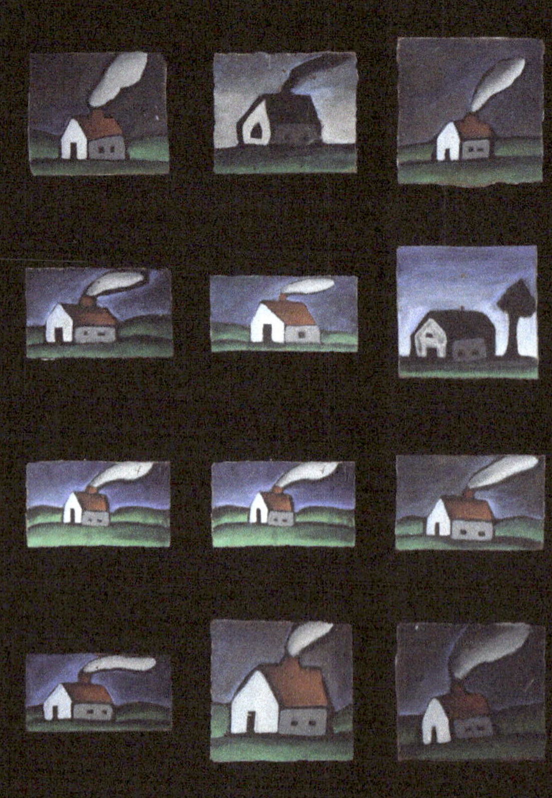

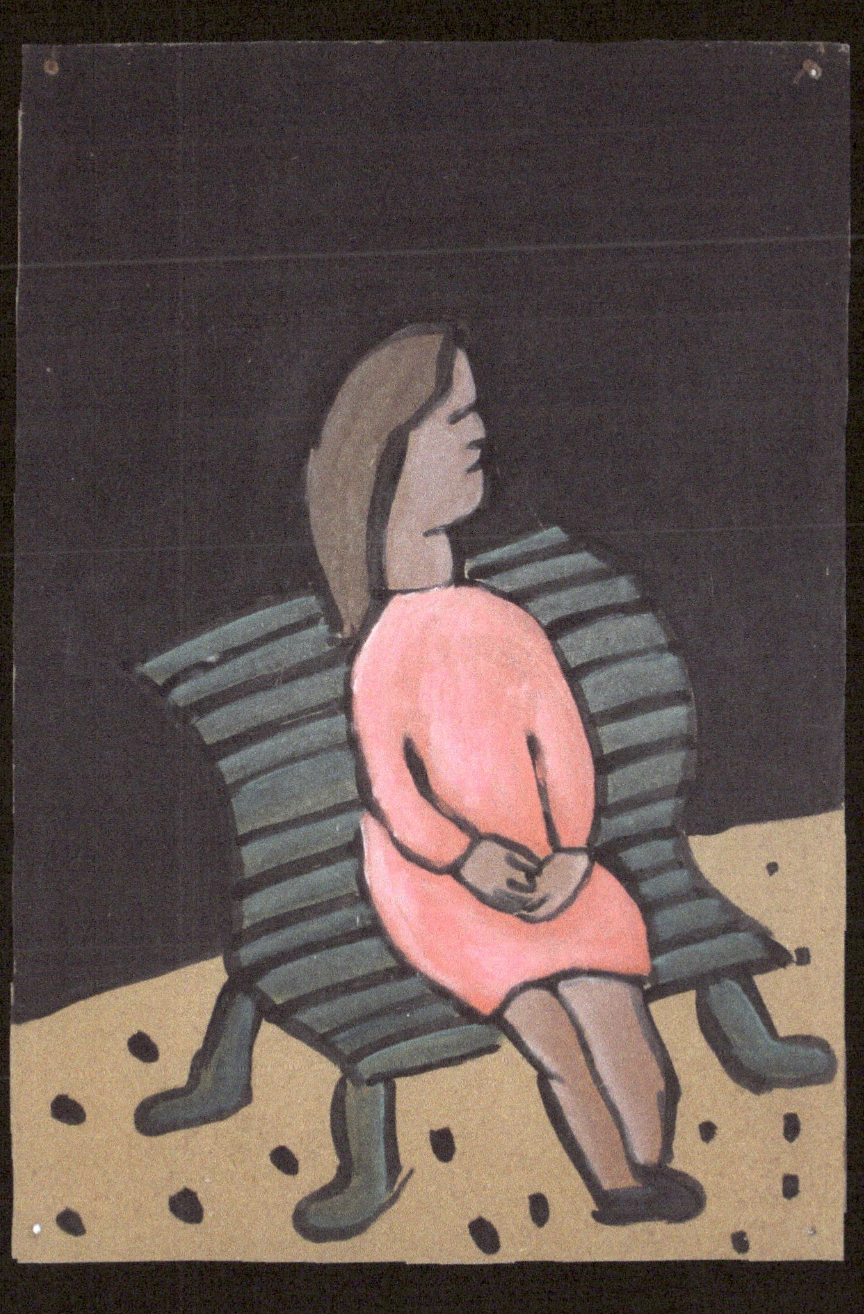

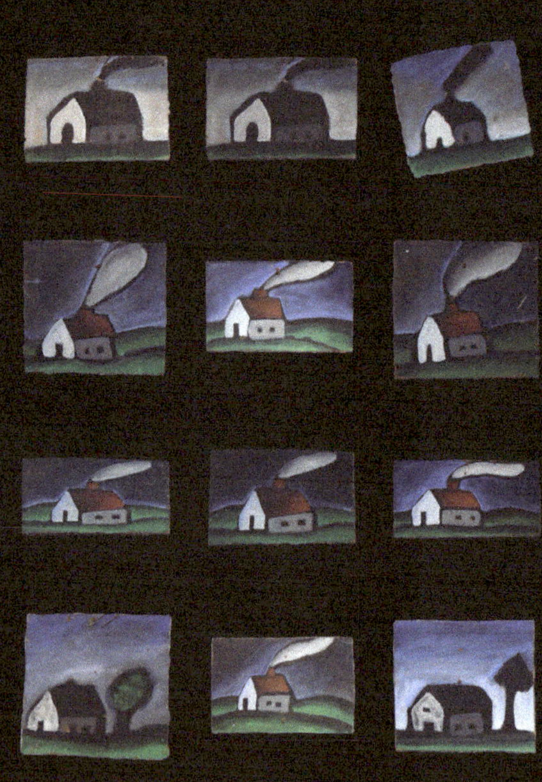

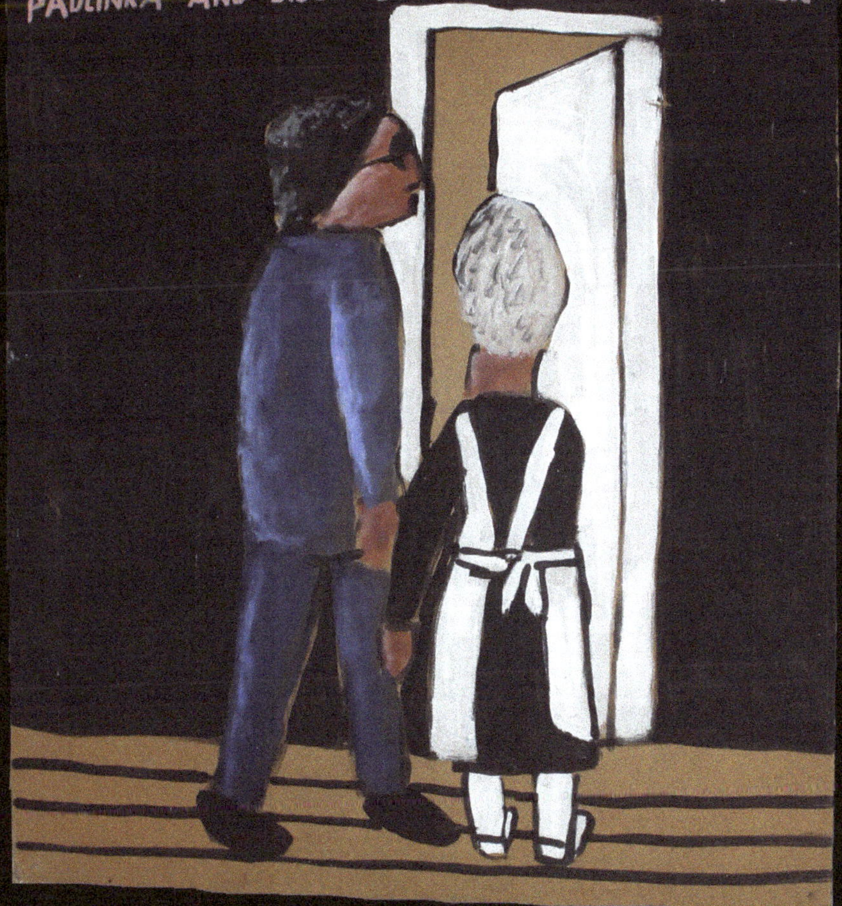
A NEW PERSON ENTERED INTO CHARLOTTE'S LIFE - DABERLOHN, A VOICE TEACHER, HE ACCOMPANIED PAULINKA AND DISCUSSED HIS THEORIES WITH HER

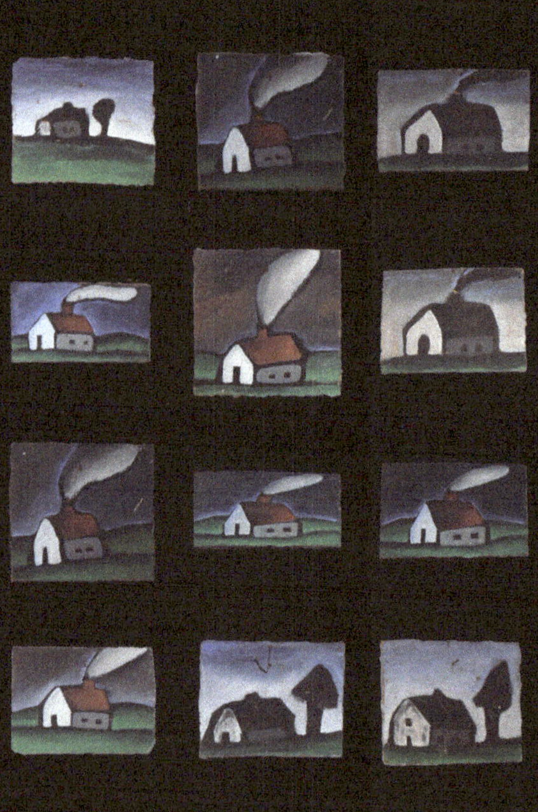

CHARLOTTE WORKED DAY AND NIGHT ON ILLUSTRATIONS

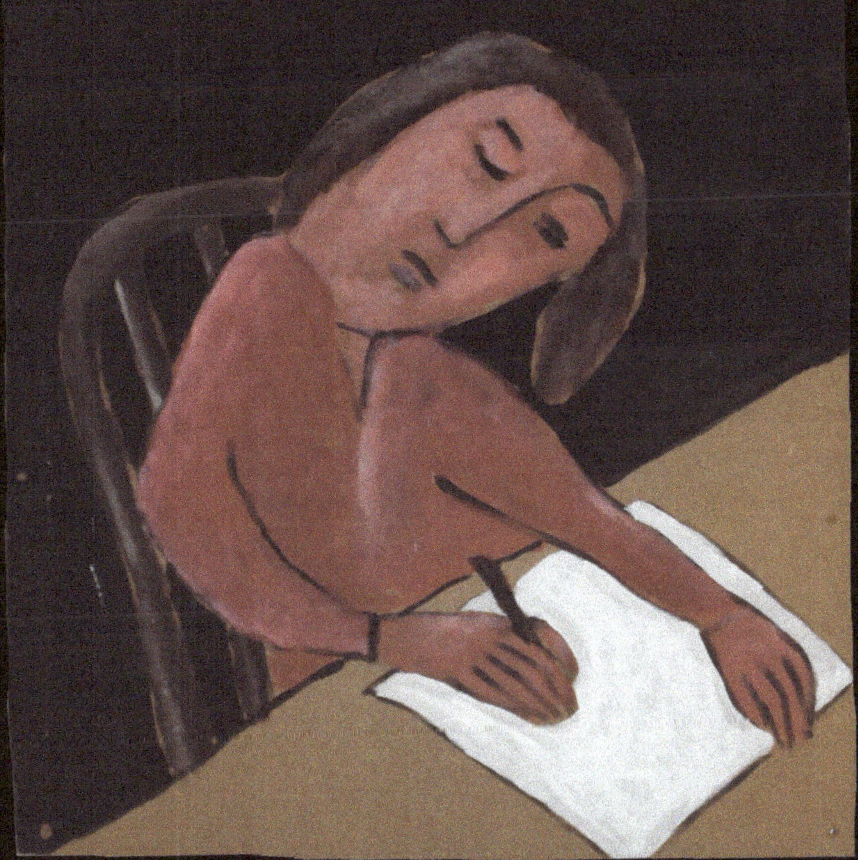

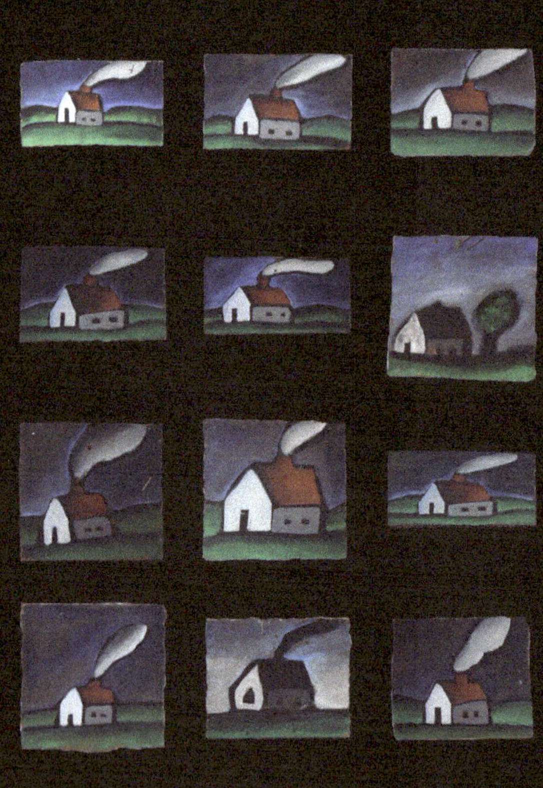

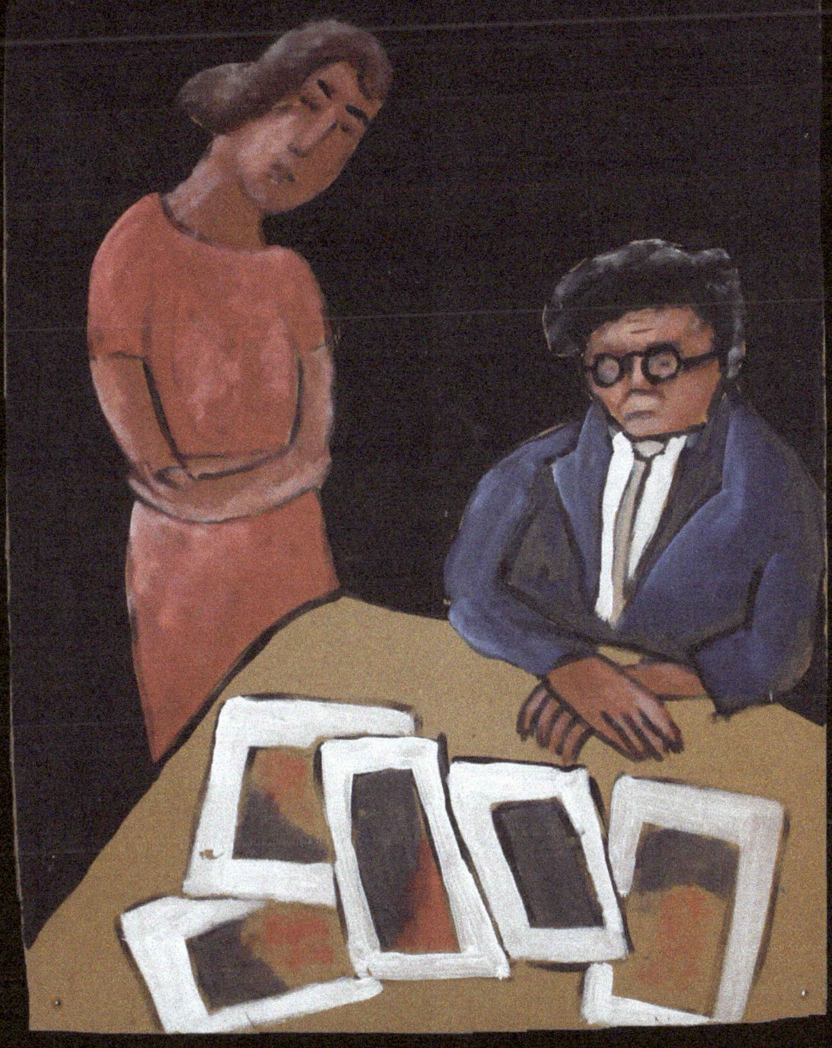
WHICH ONE WOULD YOU LIKE?

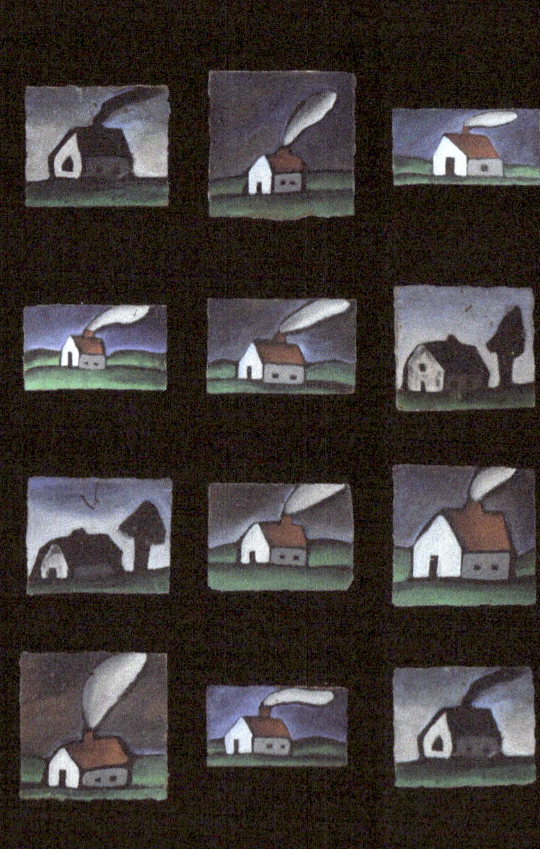

DABERLOHN TO CHARLOTTE: "I WISH EVERYONE I LOVE THE EXPERIENCE OF SUFFERING SO THAT THEY ARE FORCED TO FIND THE WAY TO THEIR DEPTHS."

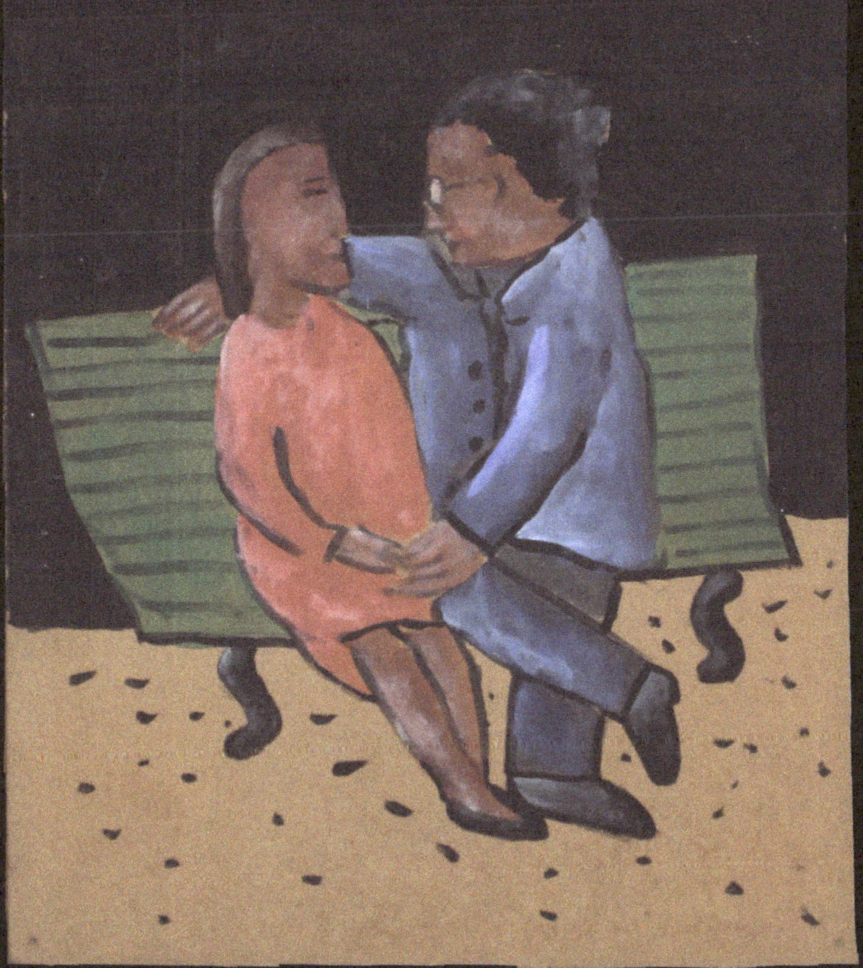

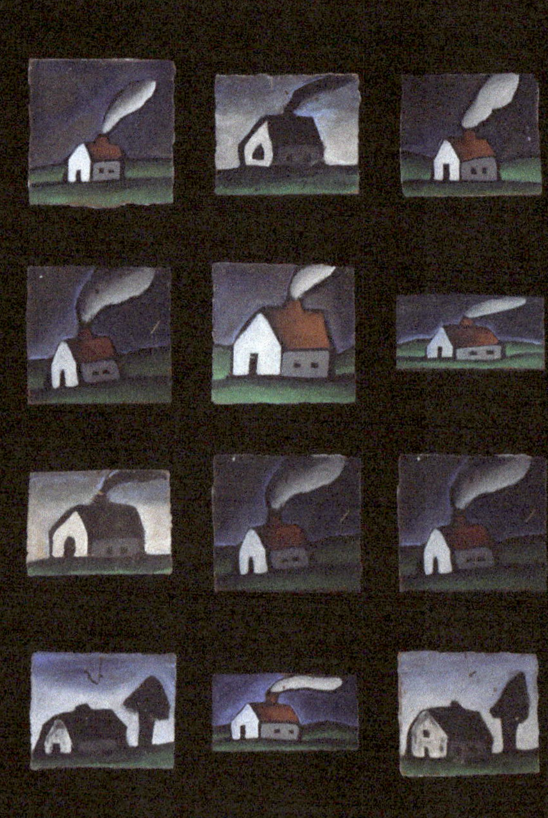

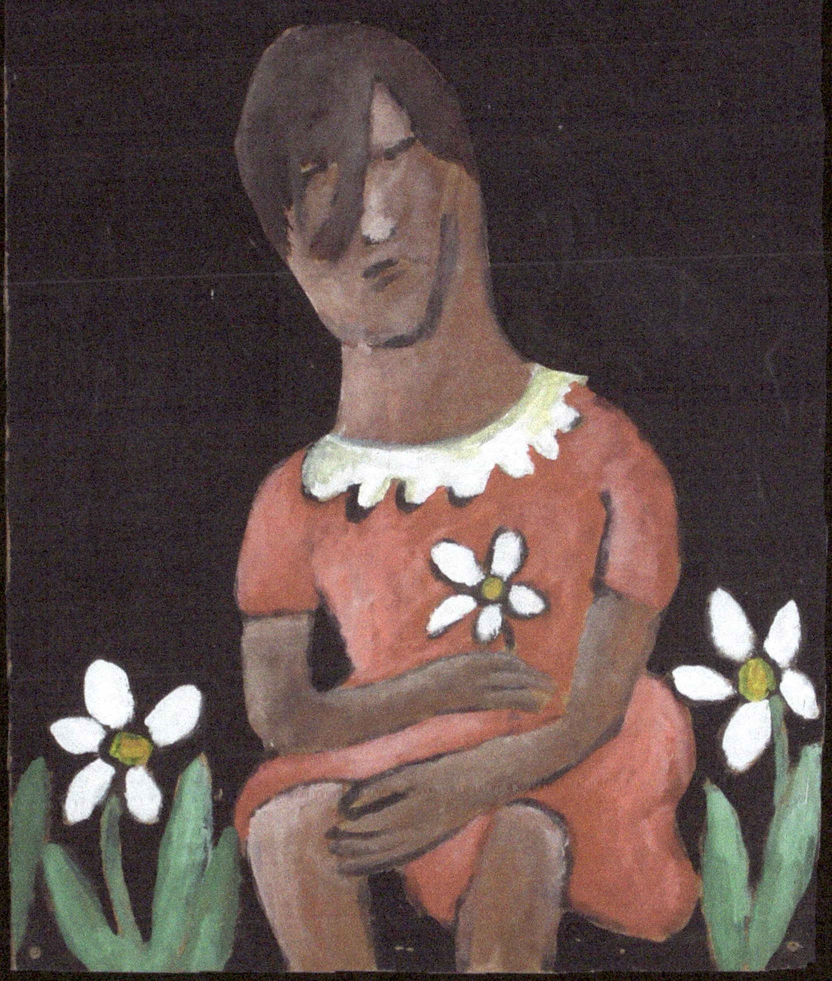
I PICKED IT FOR HIM

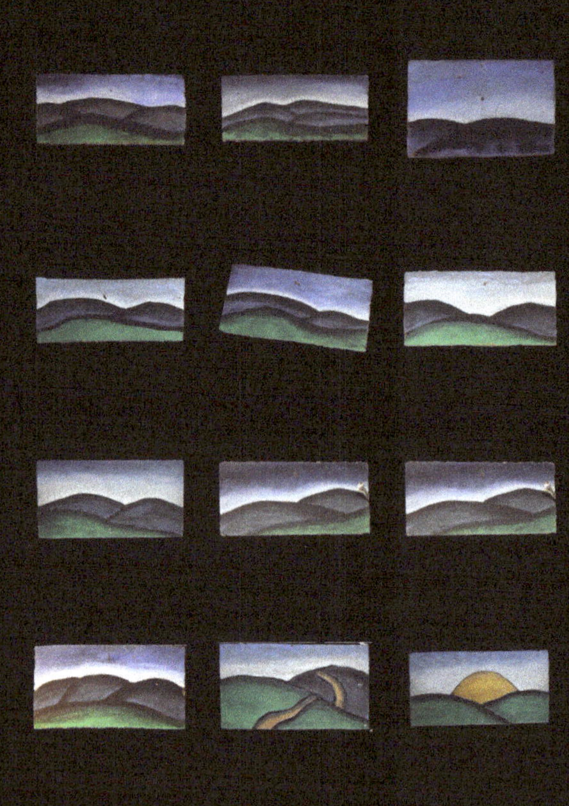

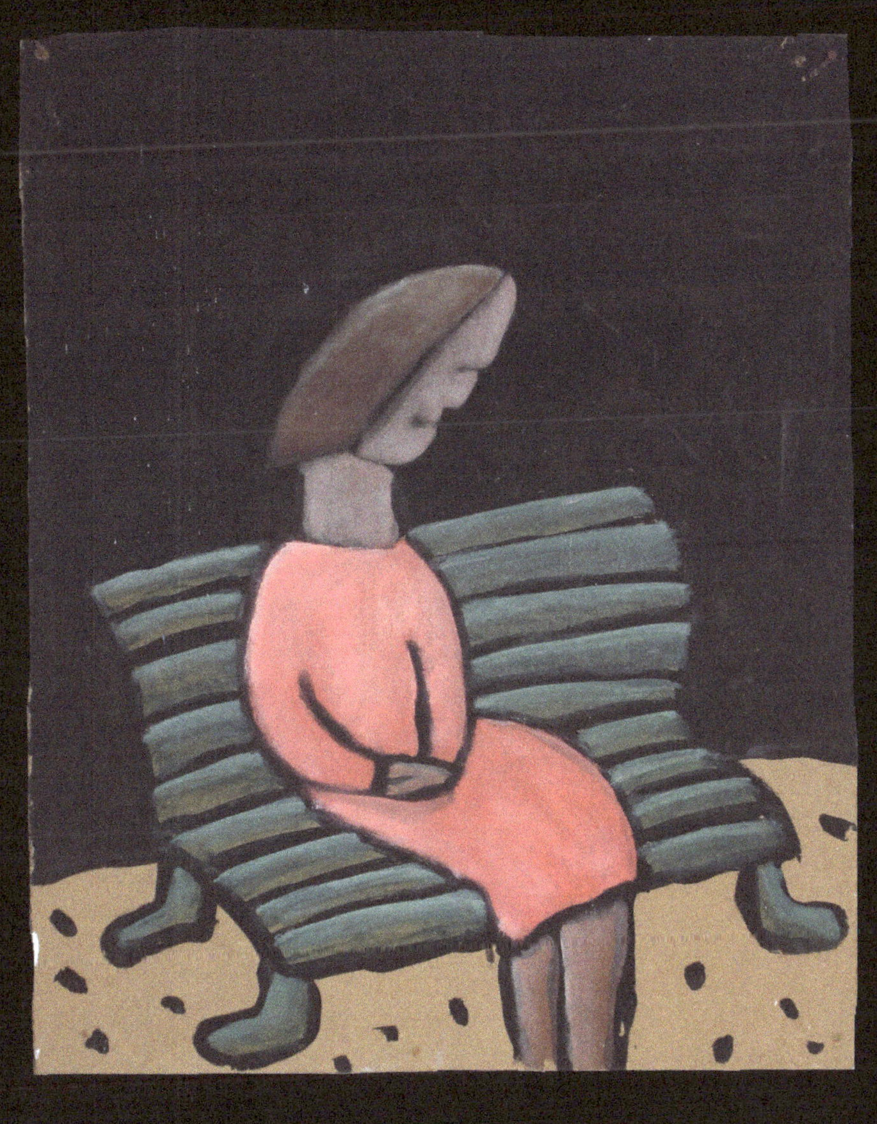

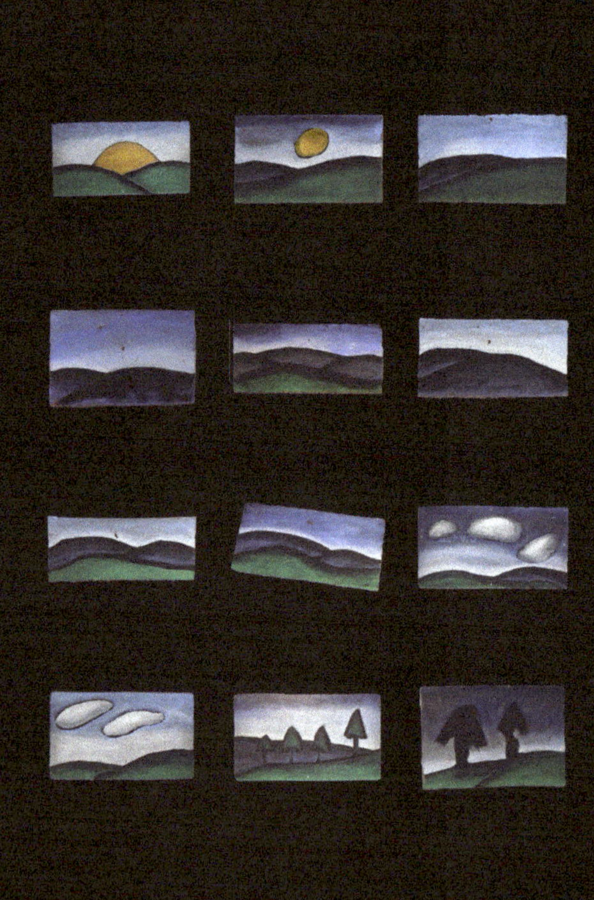

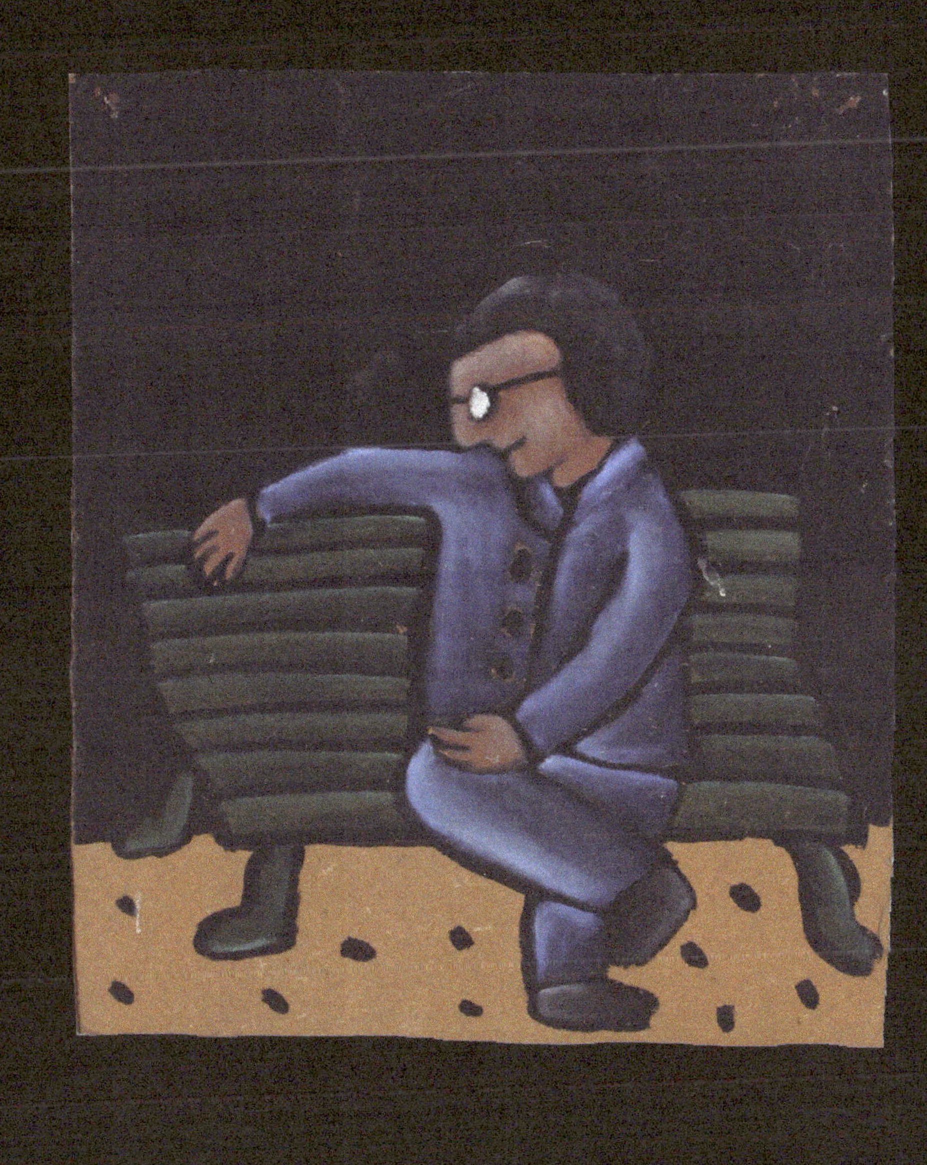

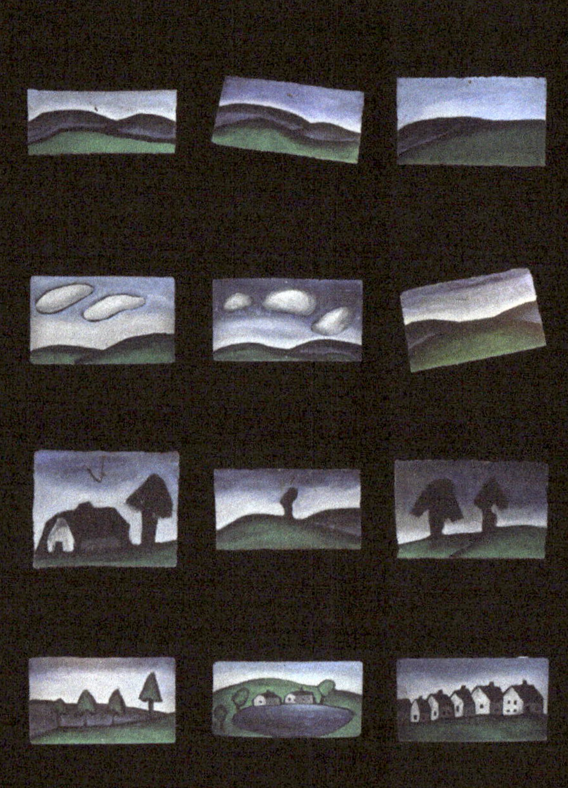

SEPTEMBER 1939.
THE GERMAN TROOPS HAVE CROSSED
THE RHINELAND BORDER.
WAR IS DECLARED.

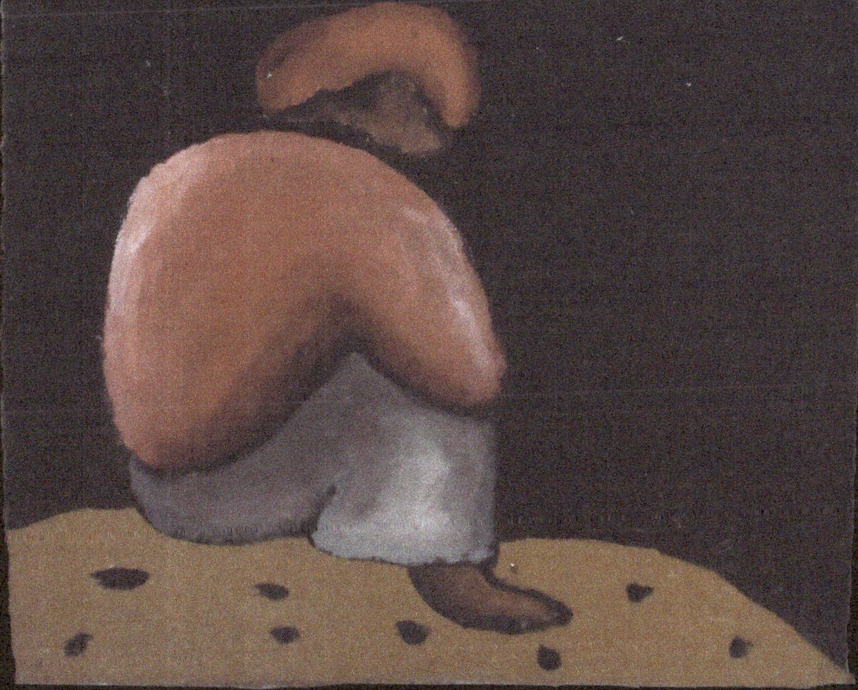

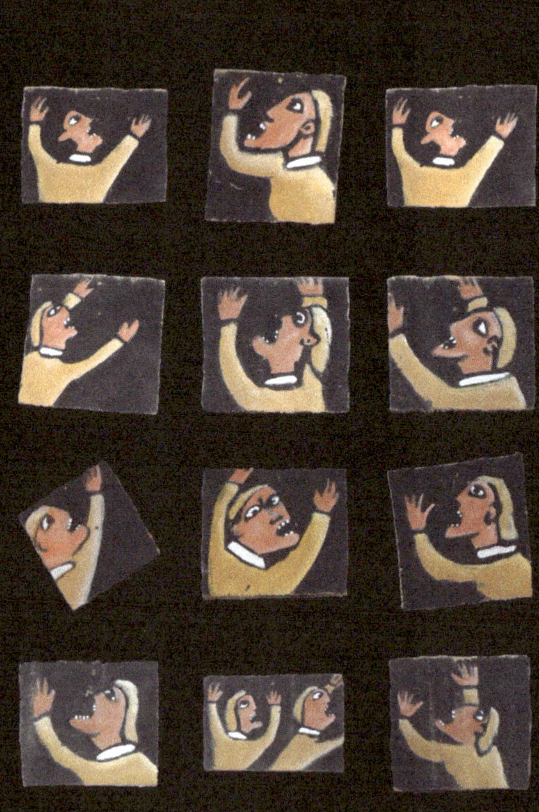

"VENGEANCE ON THE JEWS AND DESTRUCTION TO THEIR TEMPLES."

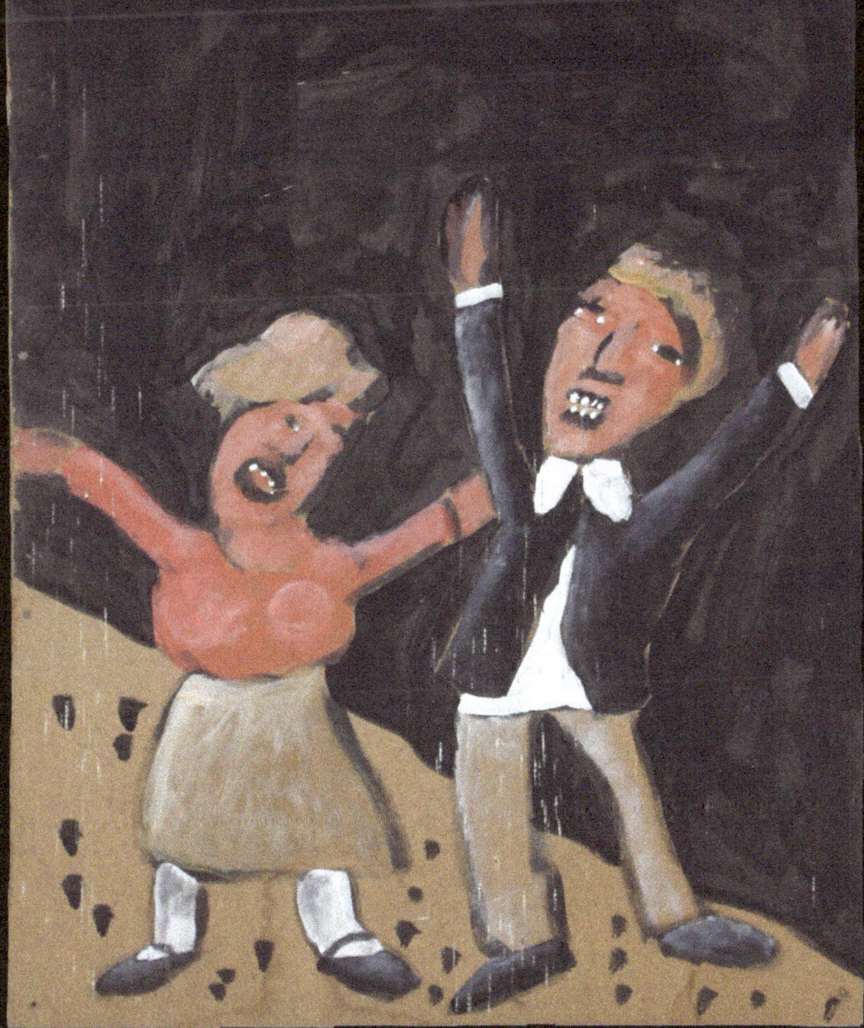

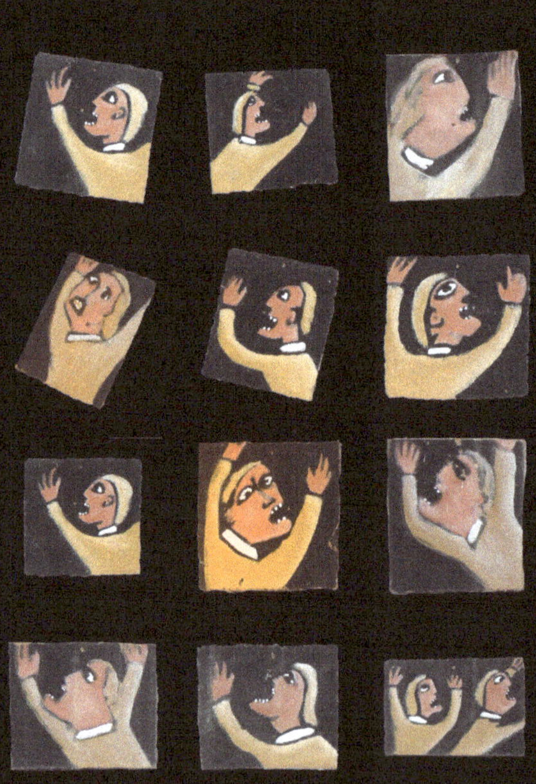

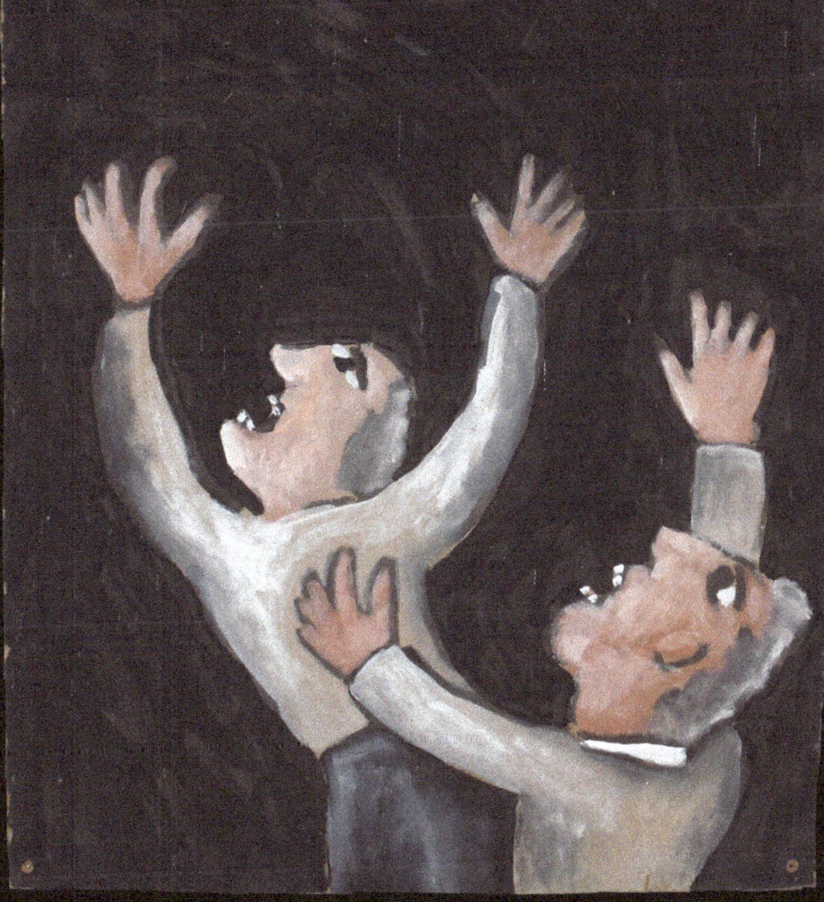
"OUT WITH THE JEWS!"

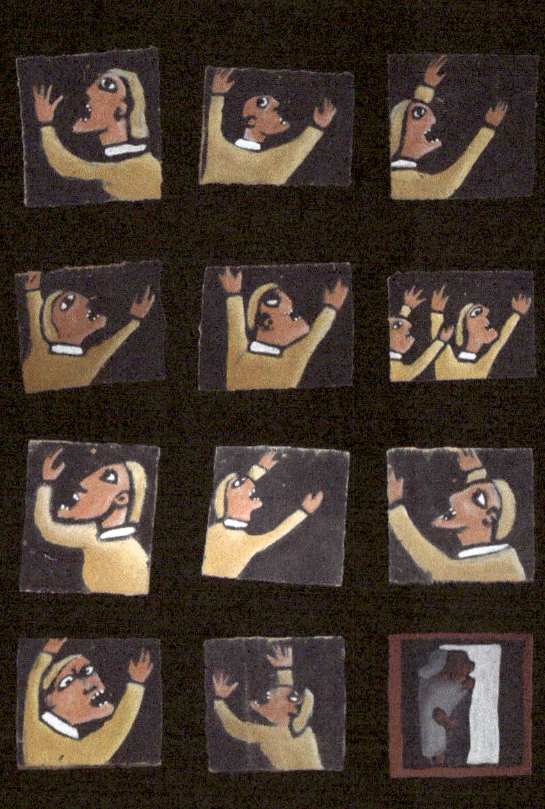

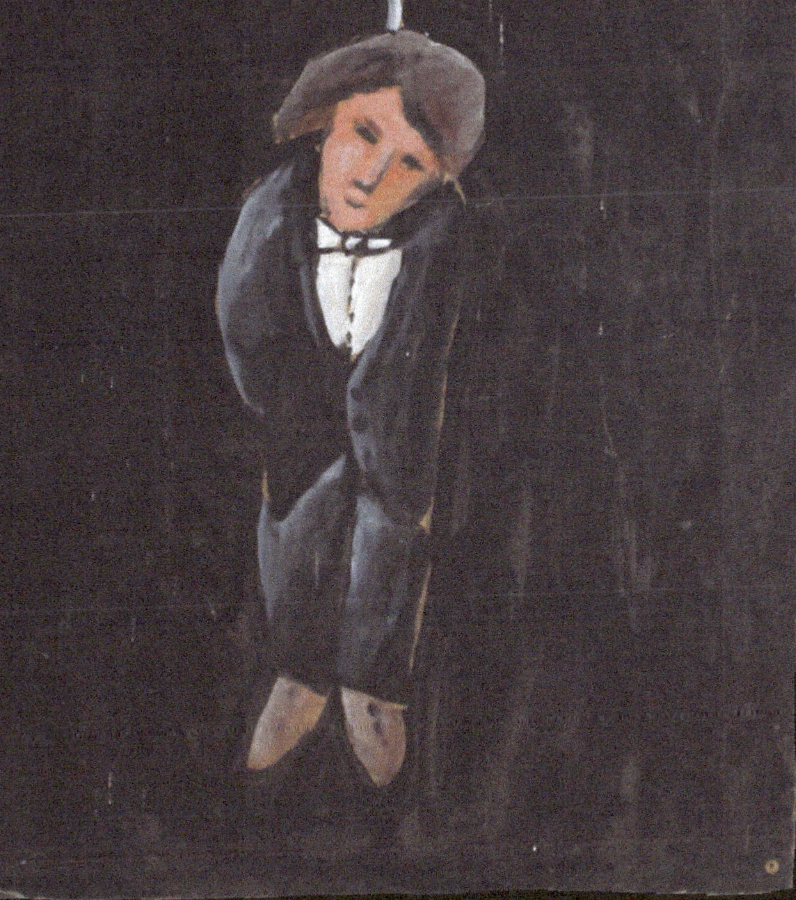
"NOW WE CAN BREATHE AGAIN, THE AIR IS CLEAR OF JEWS."

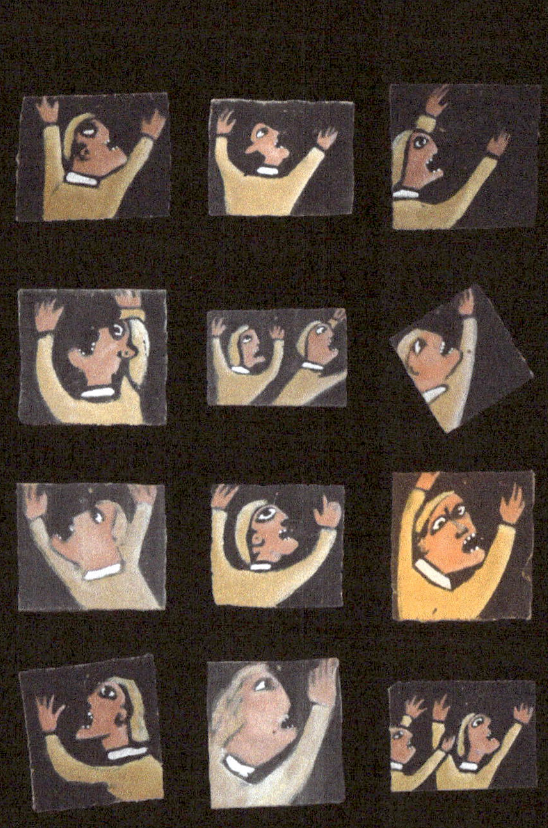

"ONE HAS TO BE ASHAMED TO BE GERMAN"

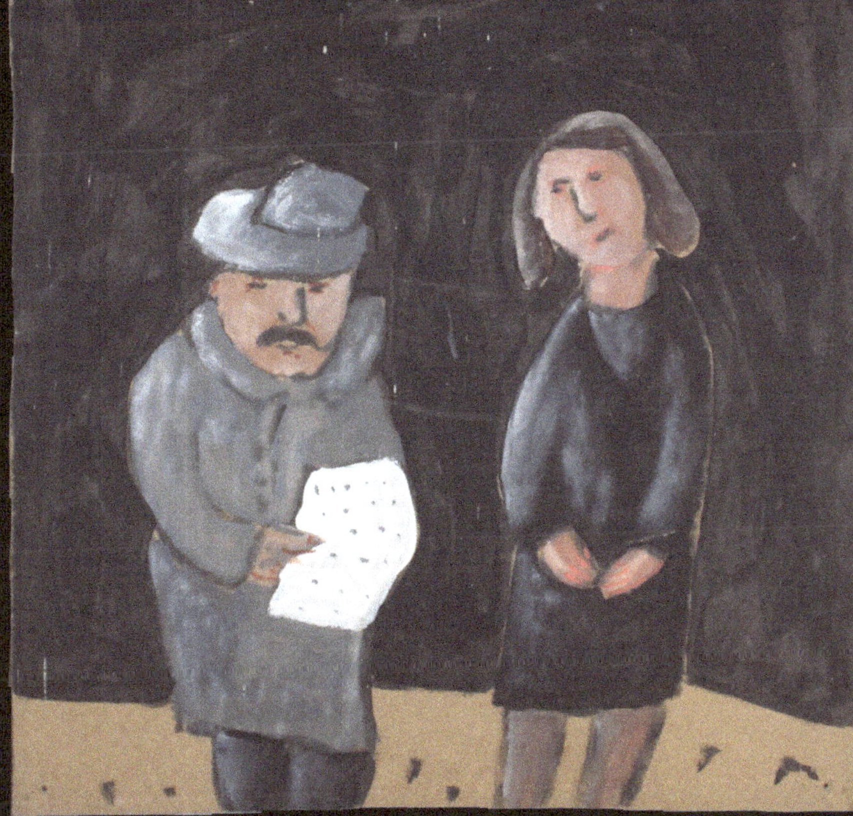

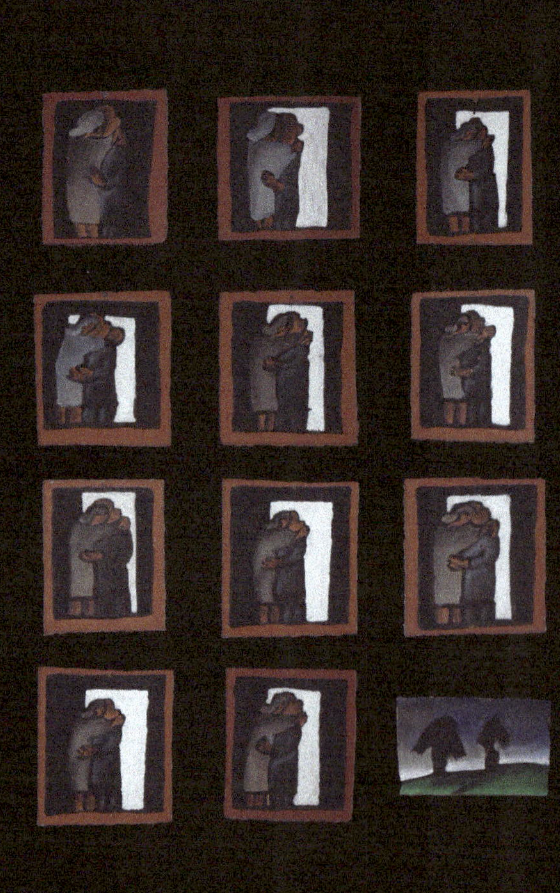

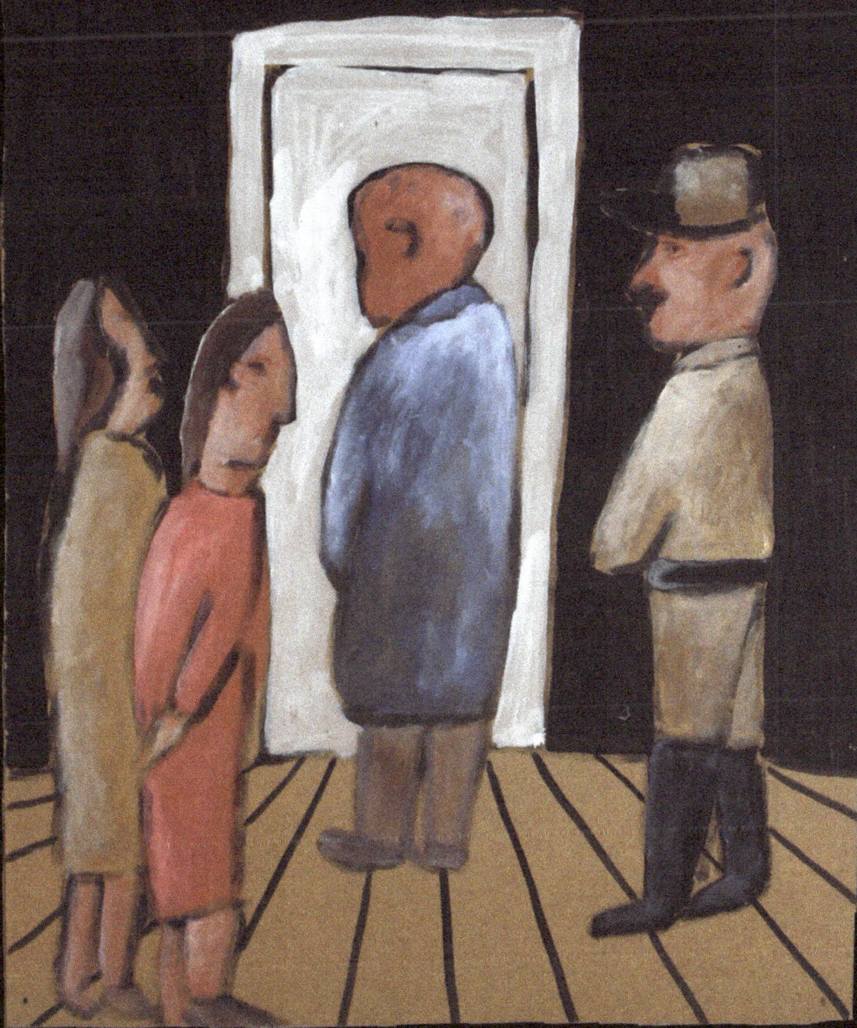
SOME TIME LATER, CHARLOTTE'S FATHER WAS TAKEN AWAY TO A CONCENTRATION CAMP

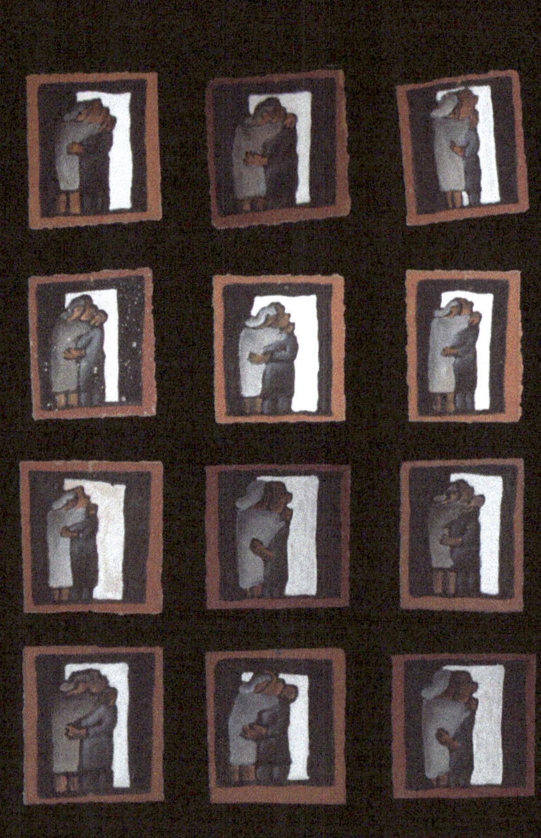

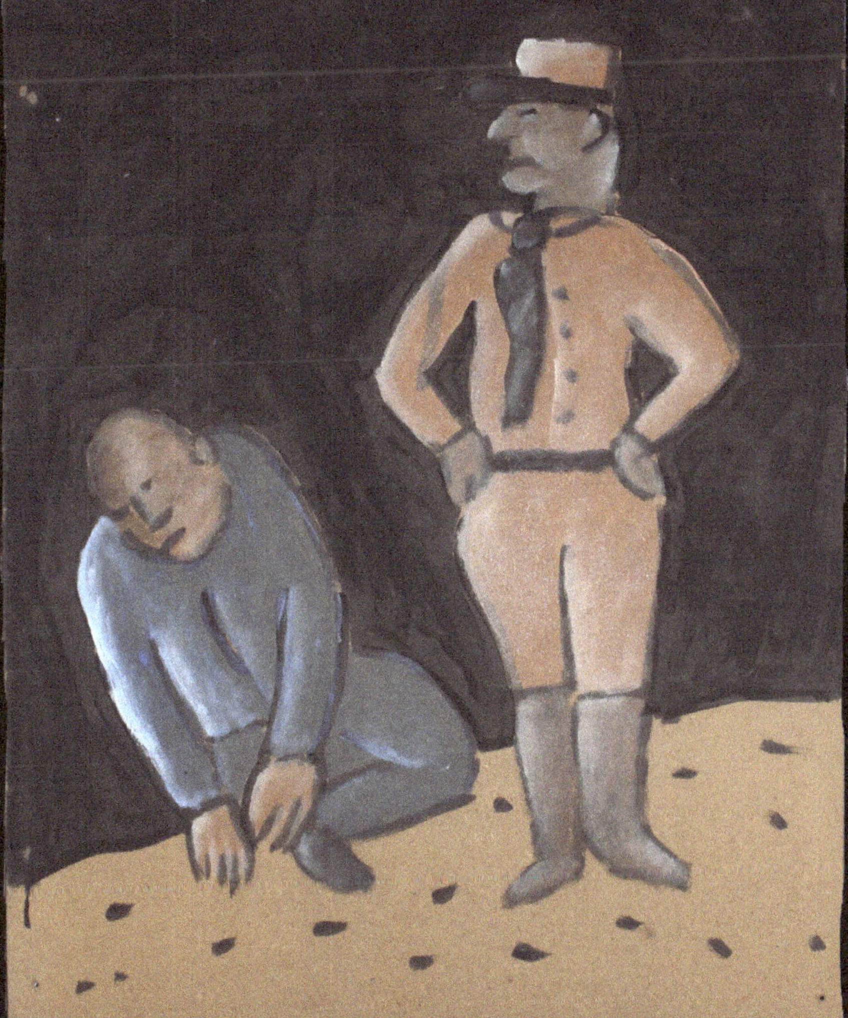
"HERE EVERYBODY HAS TO WORK!"

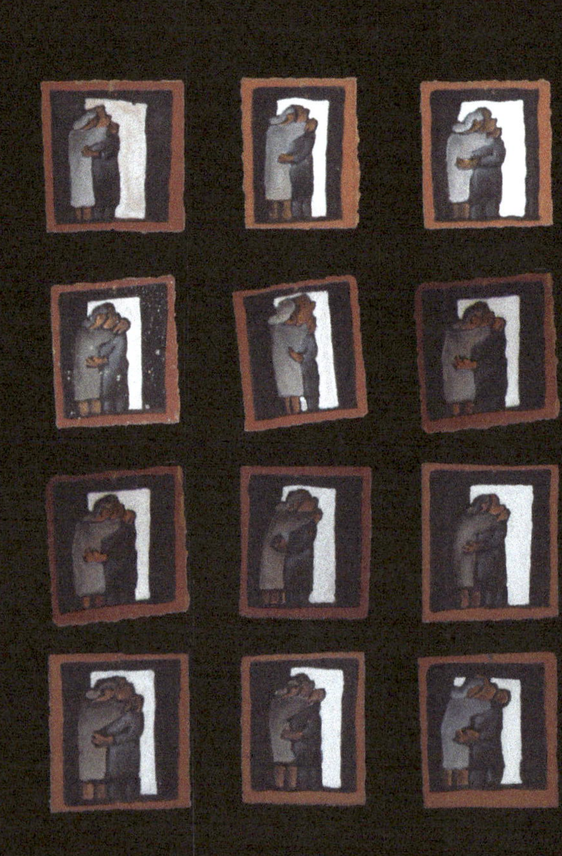

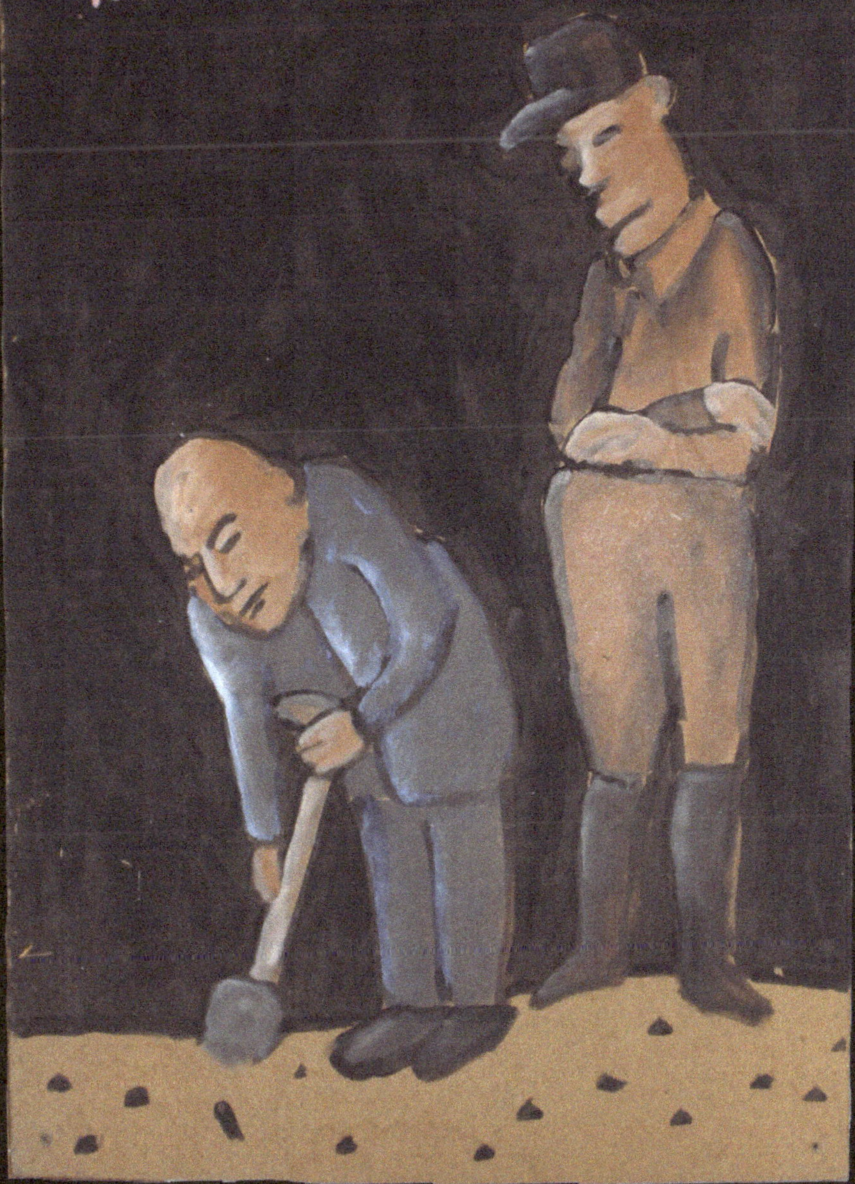
"YOU HAVE BEEN LAZY LONG ENOUGH!"

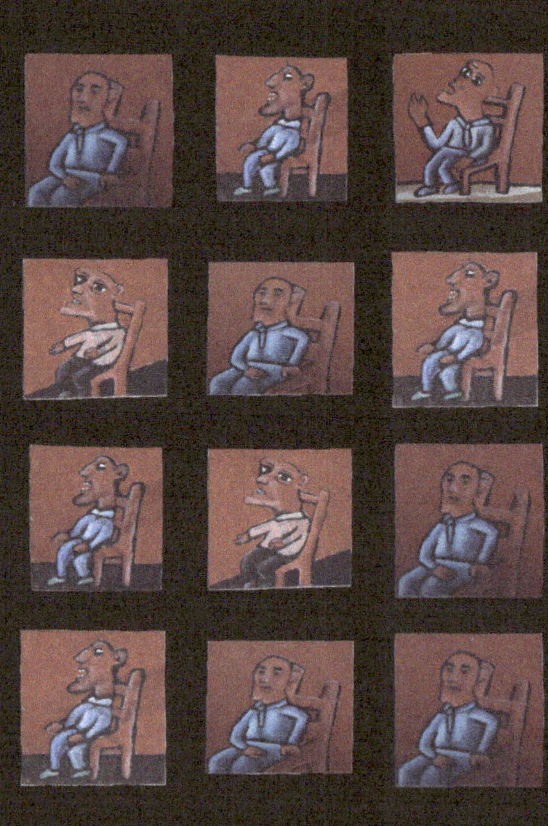

CHARLOTTE WENT TO THE POLICESTATION TO
MAKE INQUIRIES ABOUT HER FATHER. THE SQUA
WAS FILLED WITH ANXIOUS WOMEN.
"WE WANT TO KNOW WHERE OUR MEN
ARE"

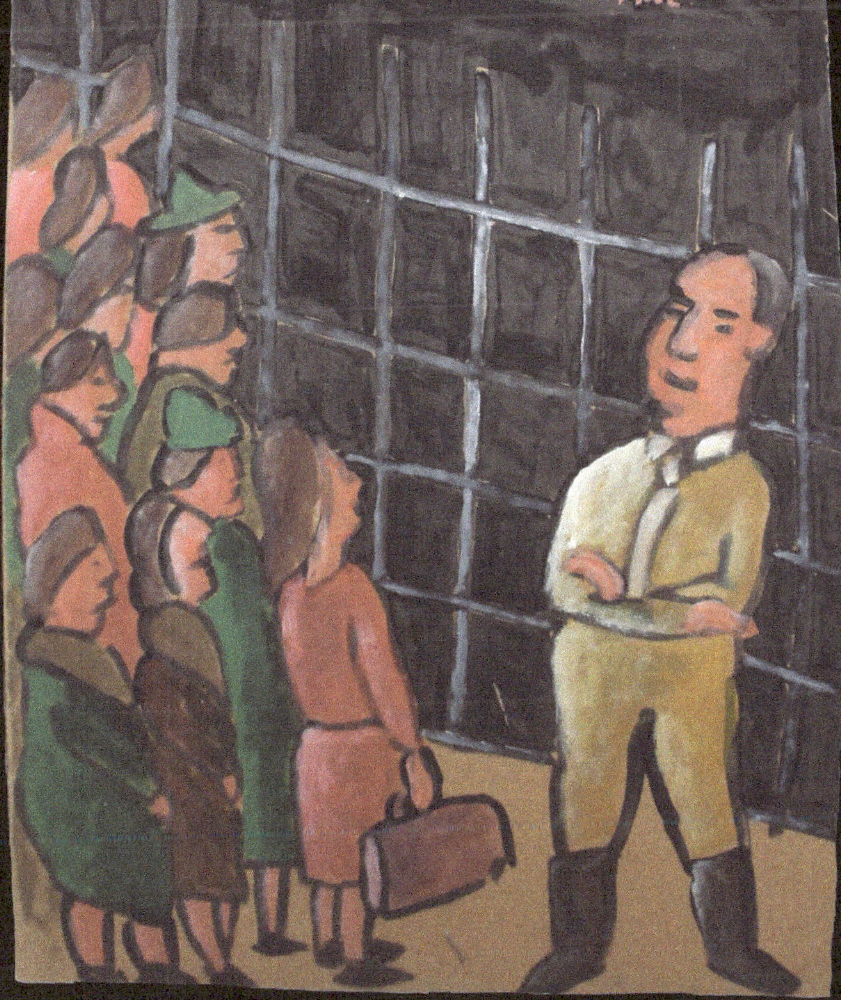

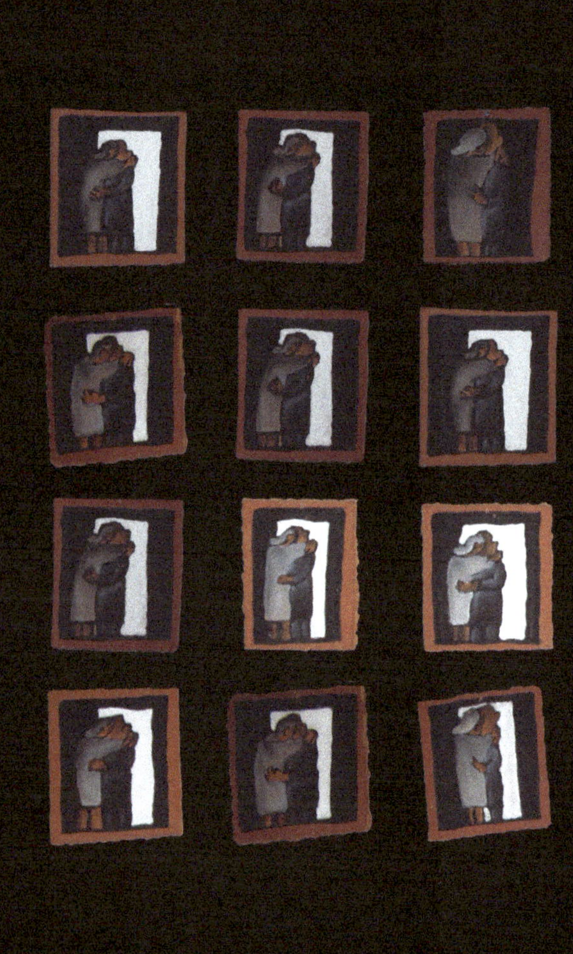

AS A SINGER, PAULINKA HAD MUCH INFLUENCE. SHE SUCCEEDED IN OBTAINING THE RELEASE OF HER HUSBAND

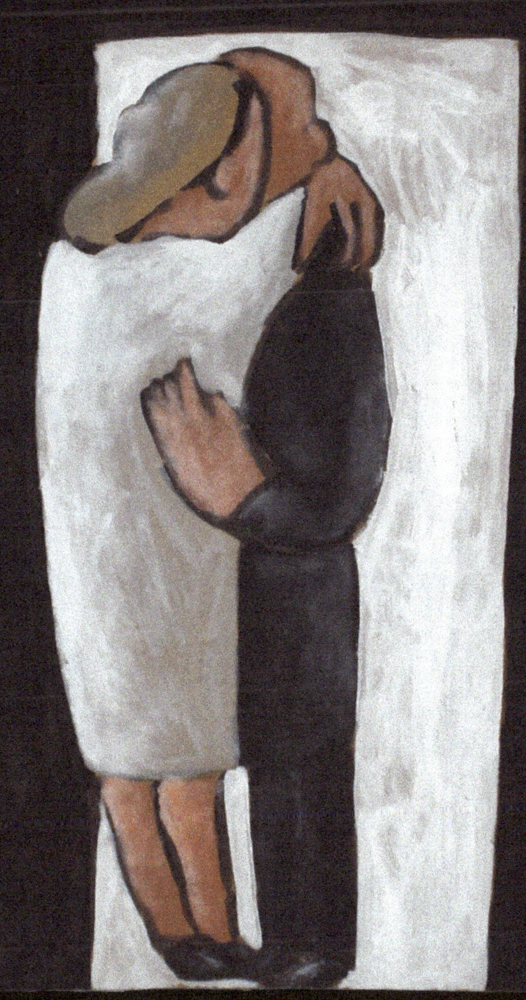

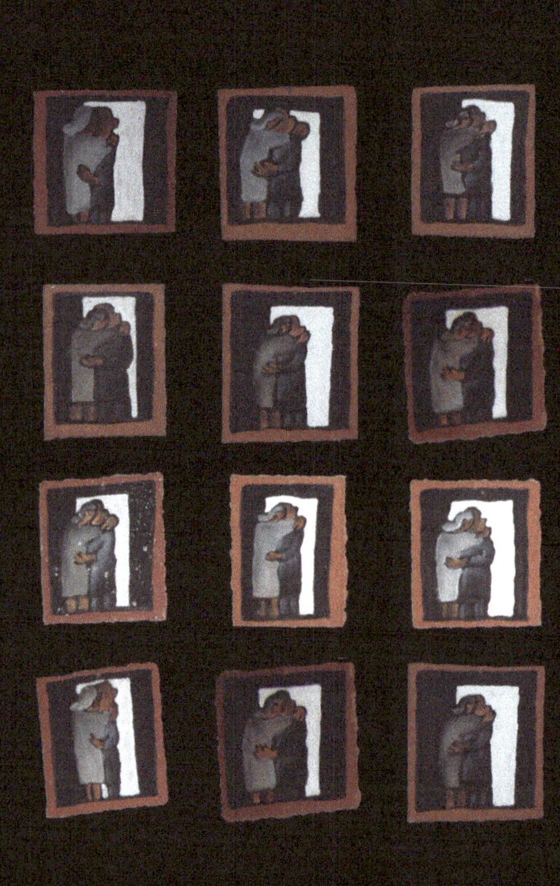

"AND HERE IS MY PICTURE TO REMEMBER ME BY."
HER FATHER SENDS CHARLOTTE TO HER GRANDPARENTS

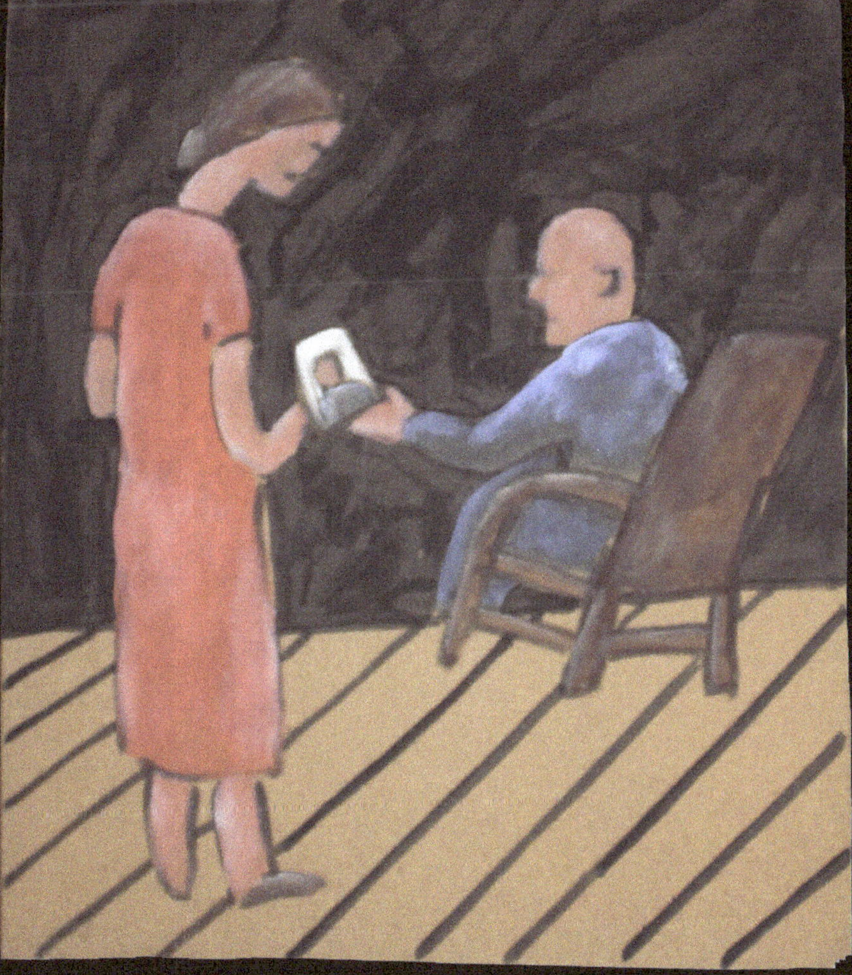

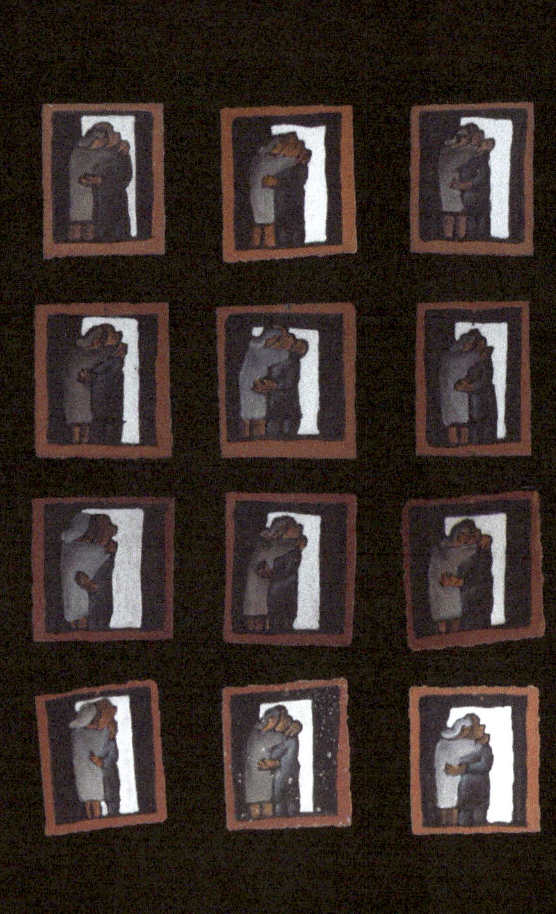

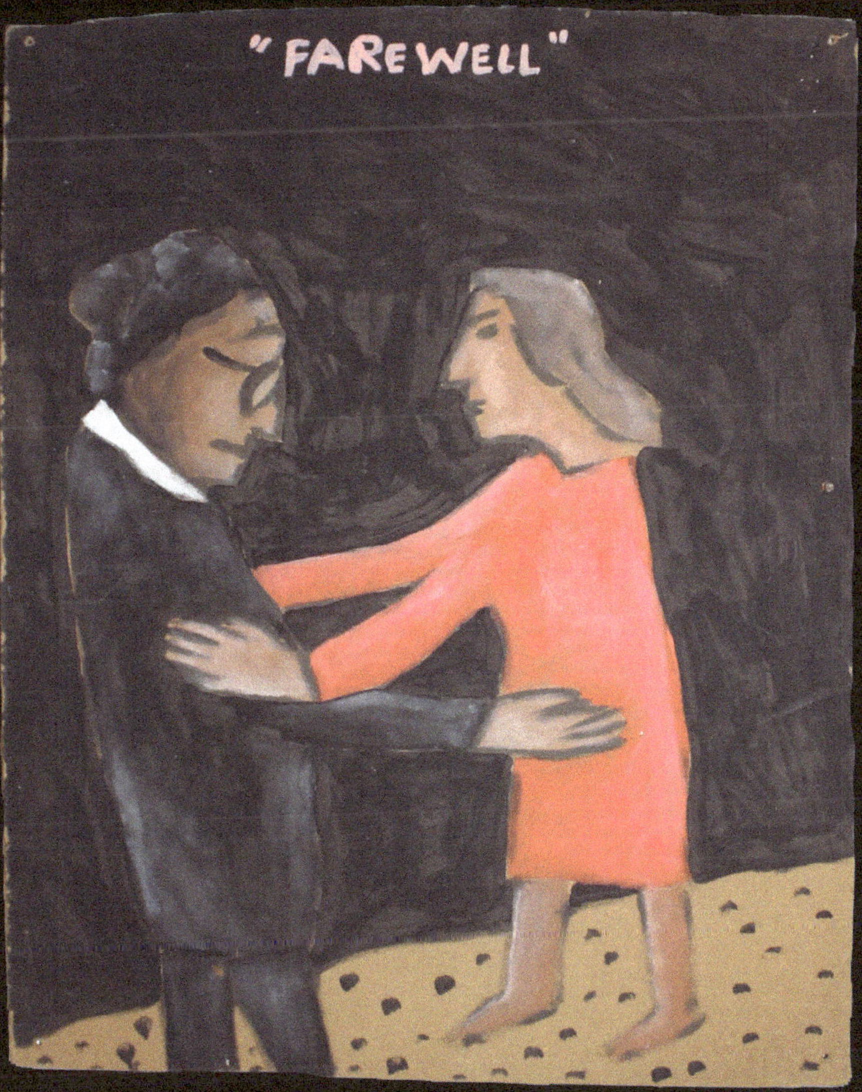

"FAREWELL"

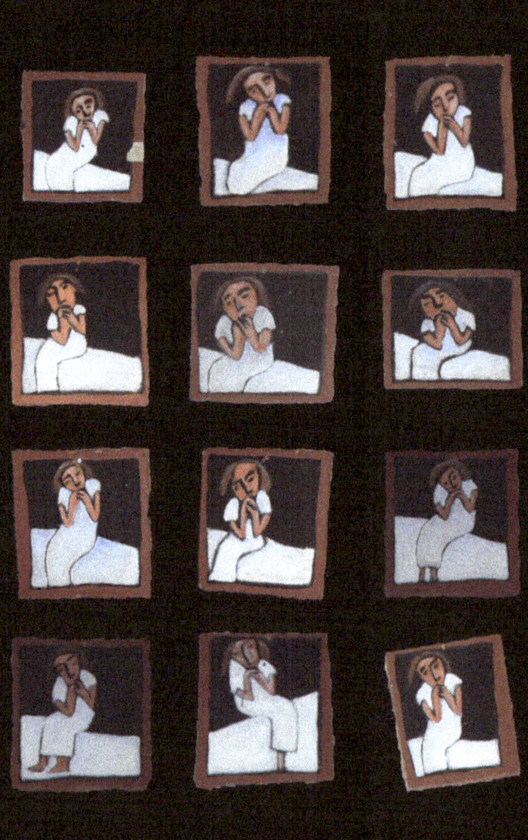

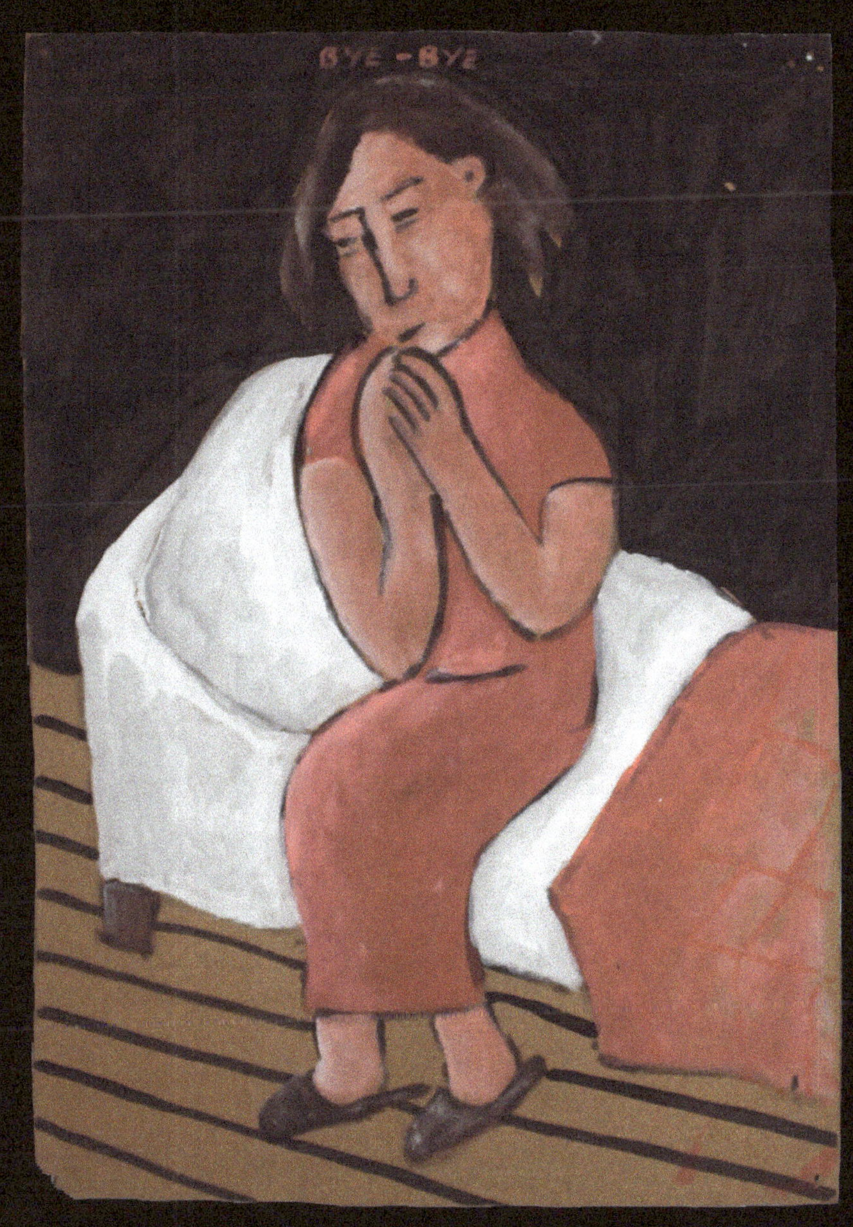
BYE-BYE

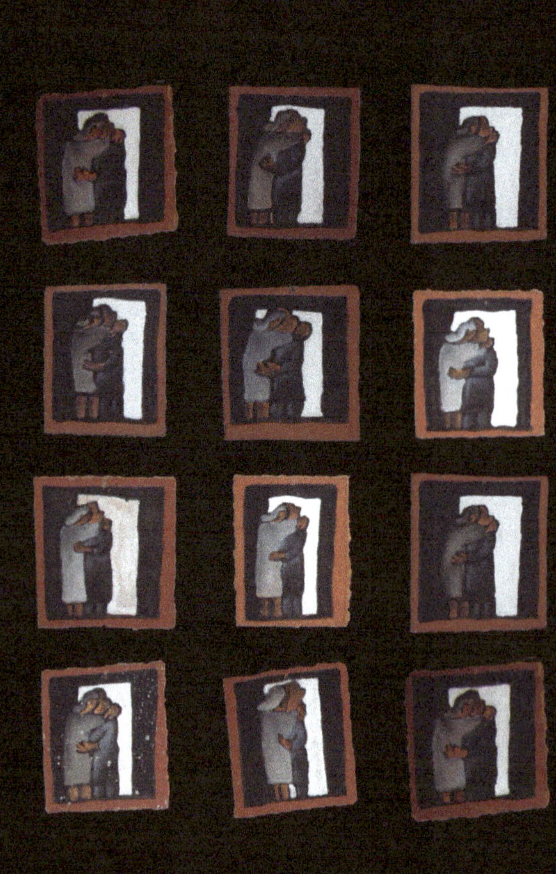

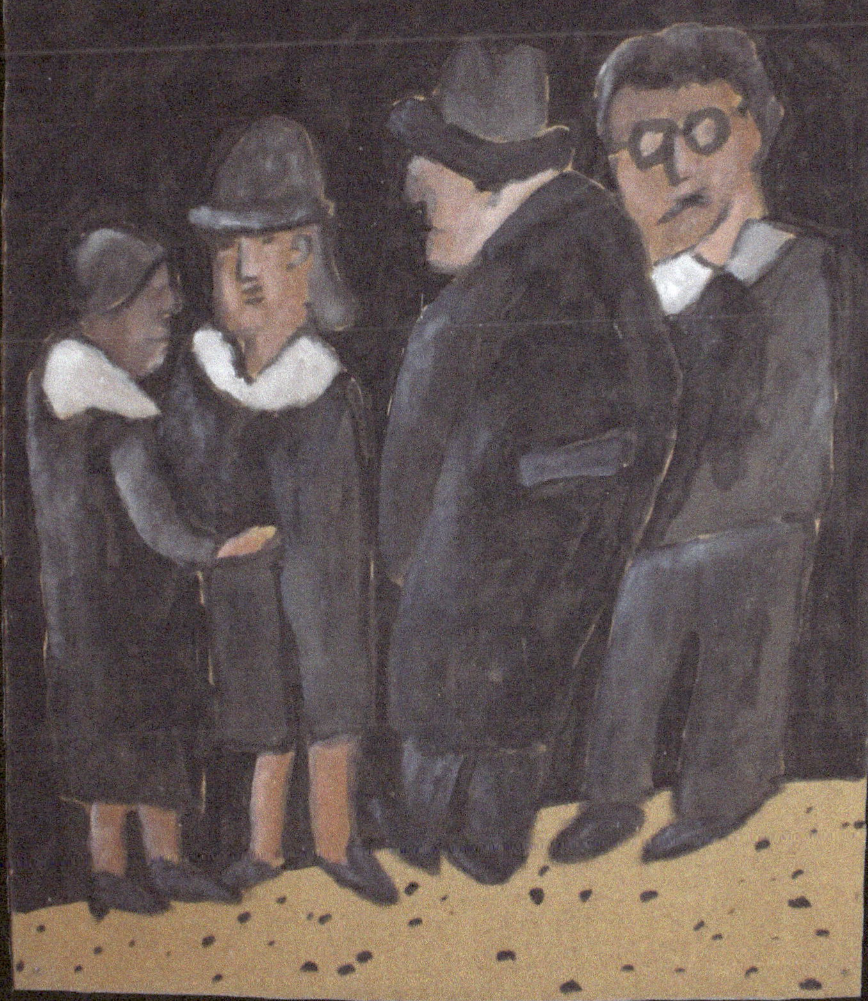
"YOU HAVE TO GO NOW"

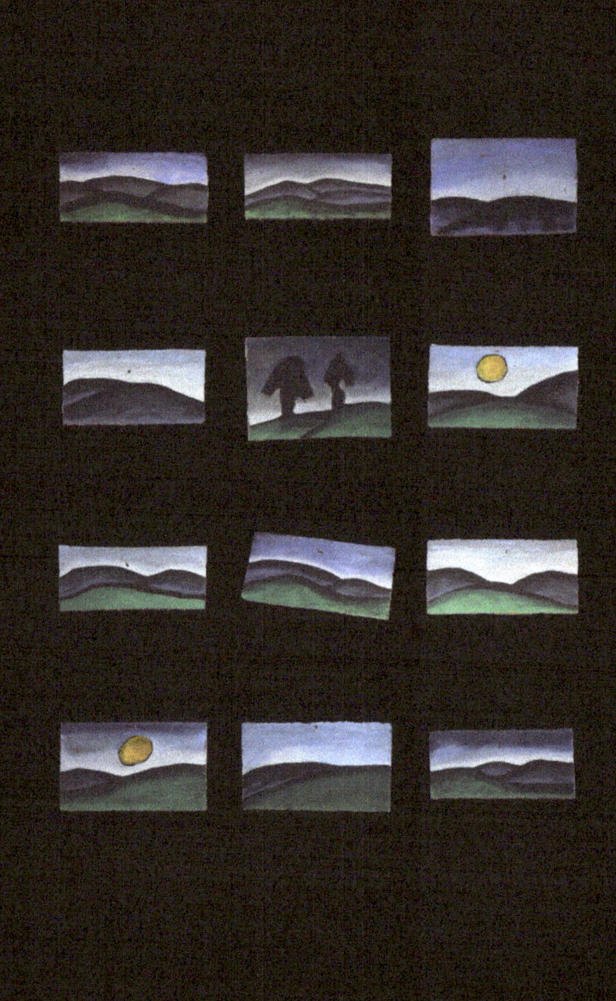

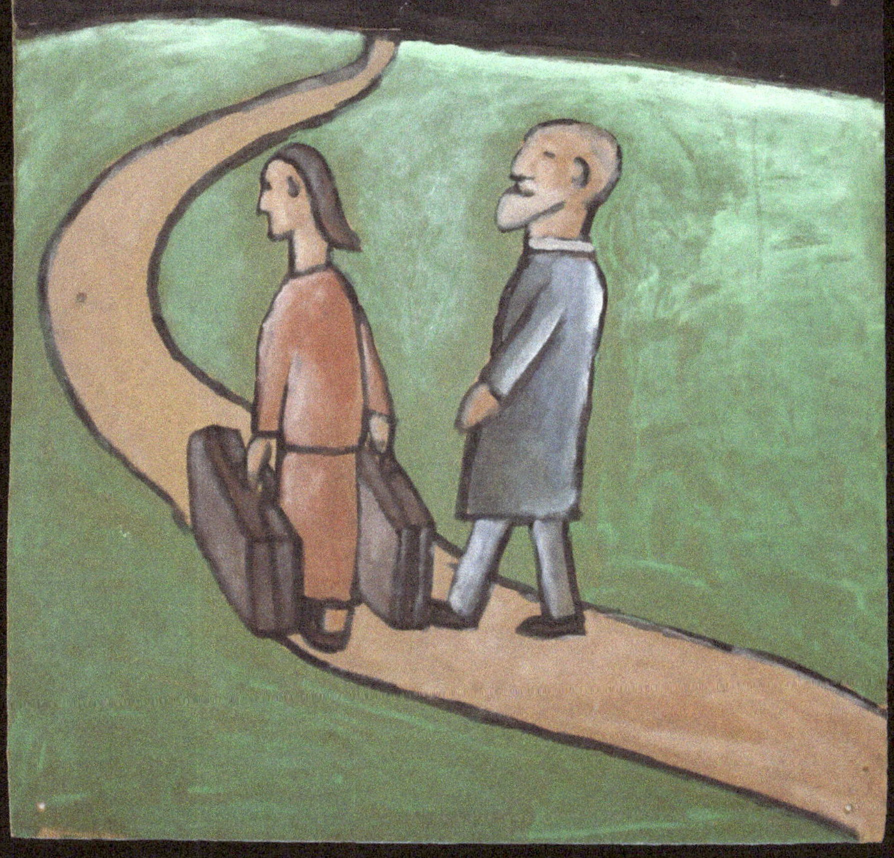
ON THE ROAD
"GOD, HOW BEAUTIFUL IT IS HERE!"

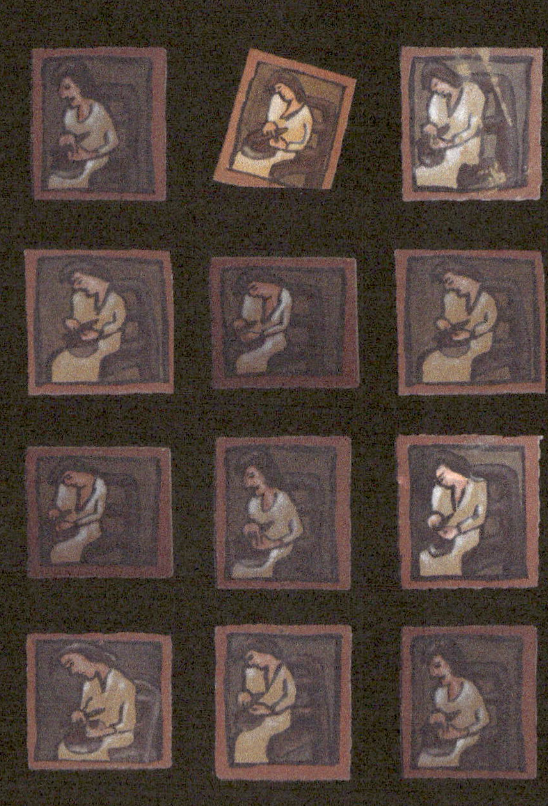

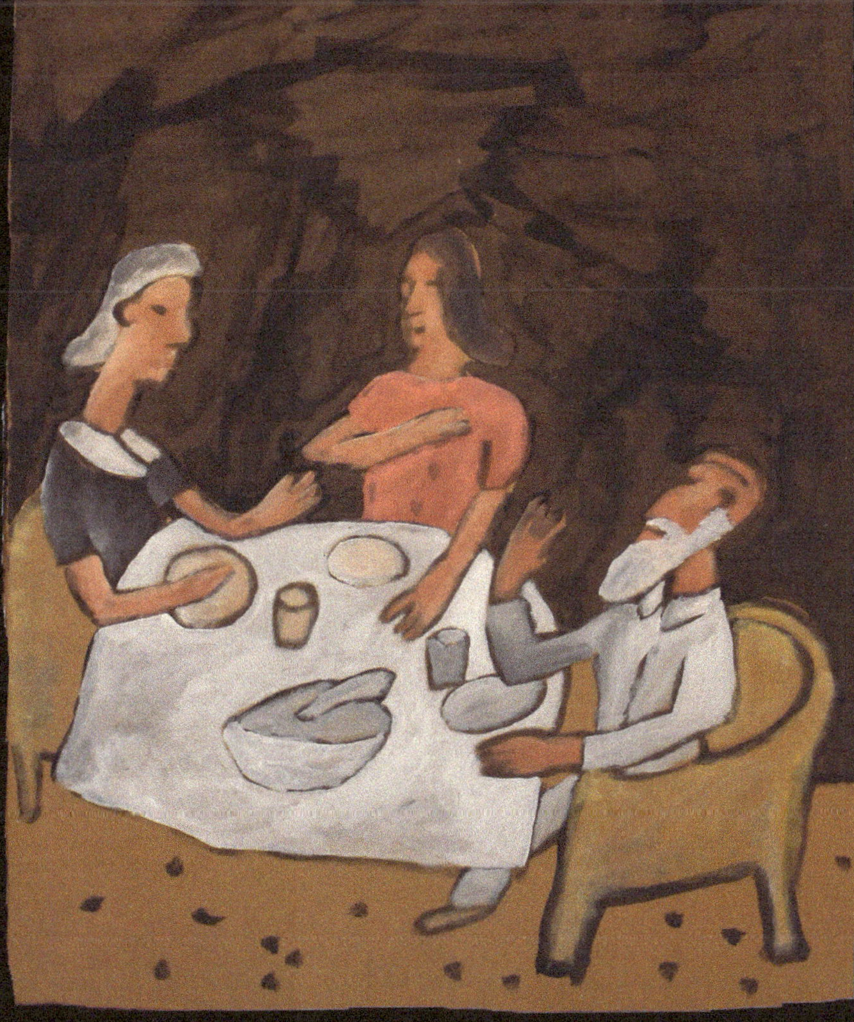
LIFE WITH THE GRANDPARENTS IS
NOT EASY

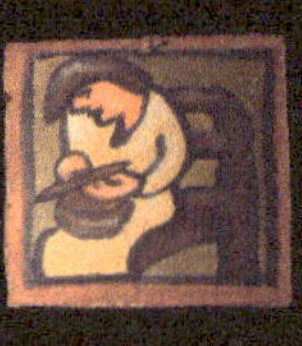
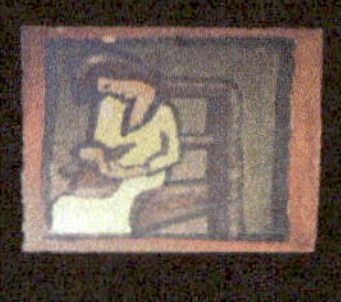
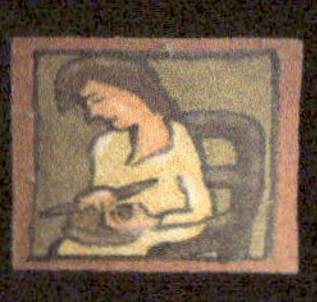
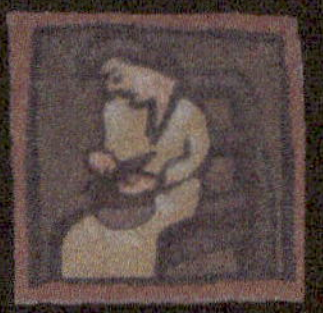
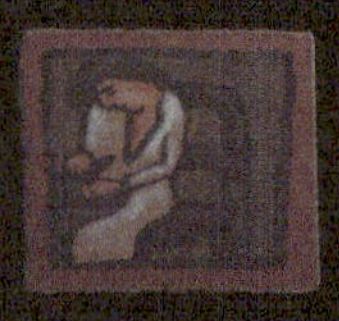
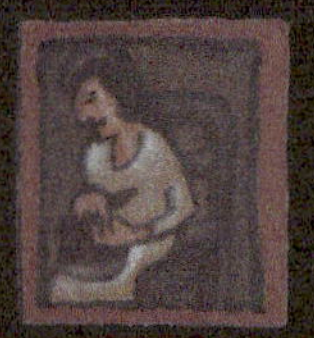
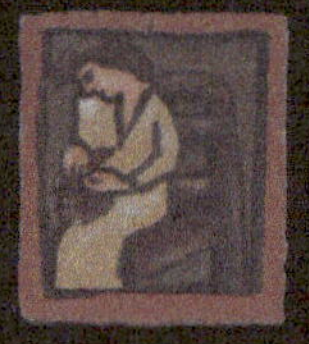
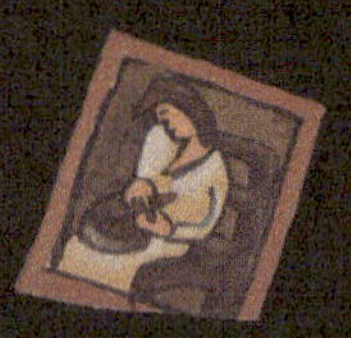
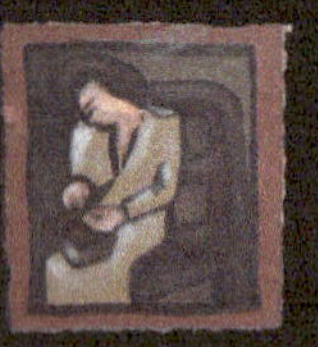
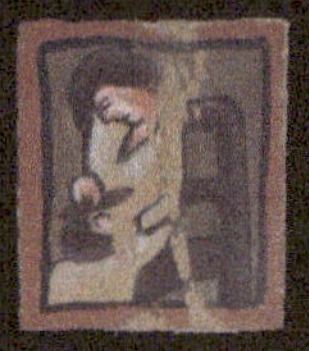
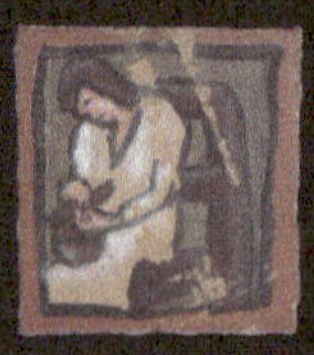
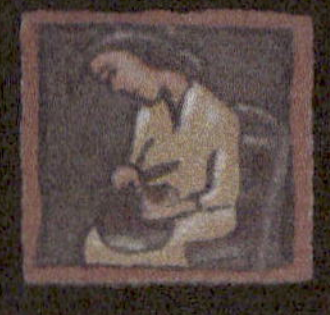

GRANDMOTHER SAYS: "JUST LOOK AT HER – ISN'T SHE MELANCHOLY PERSONIFIED?"

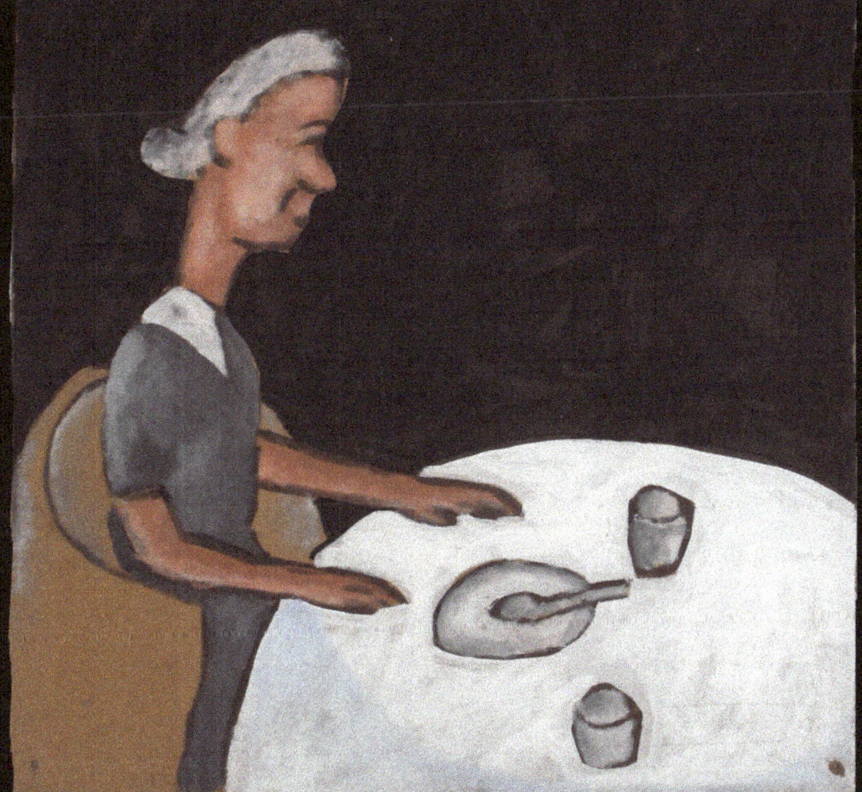

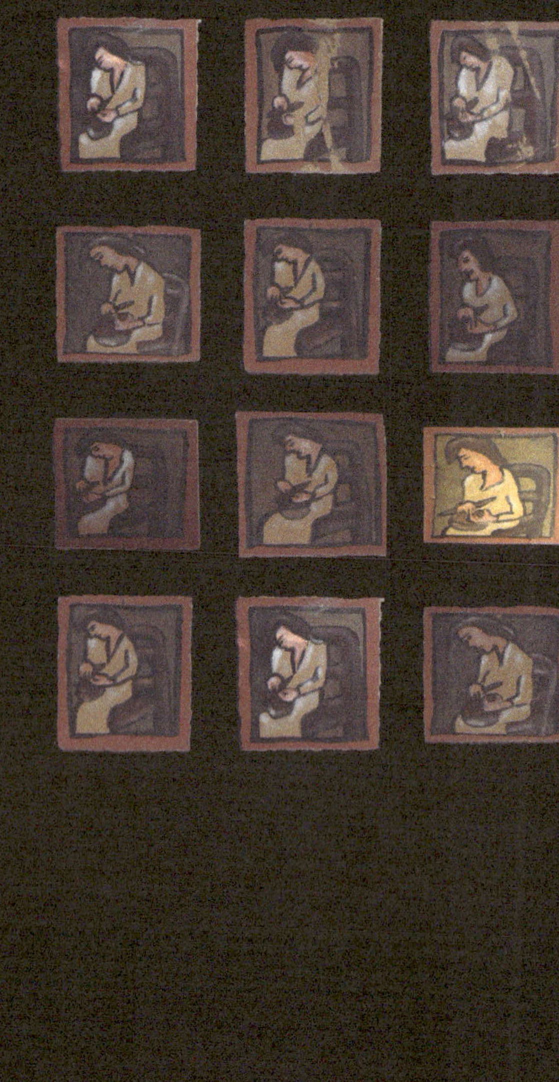

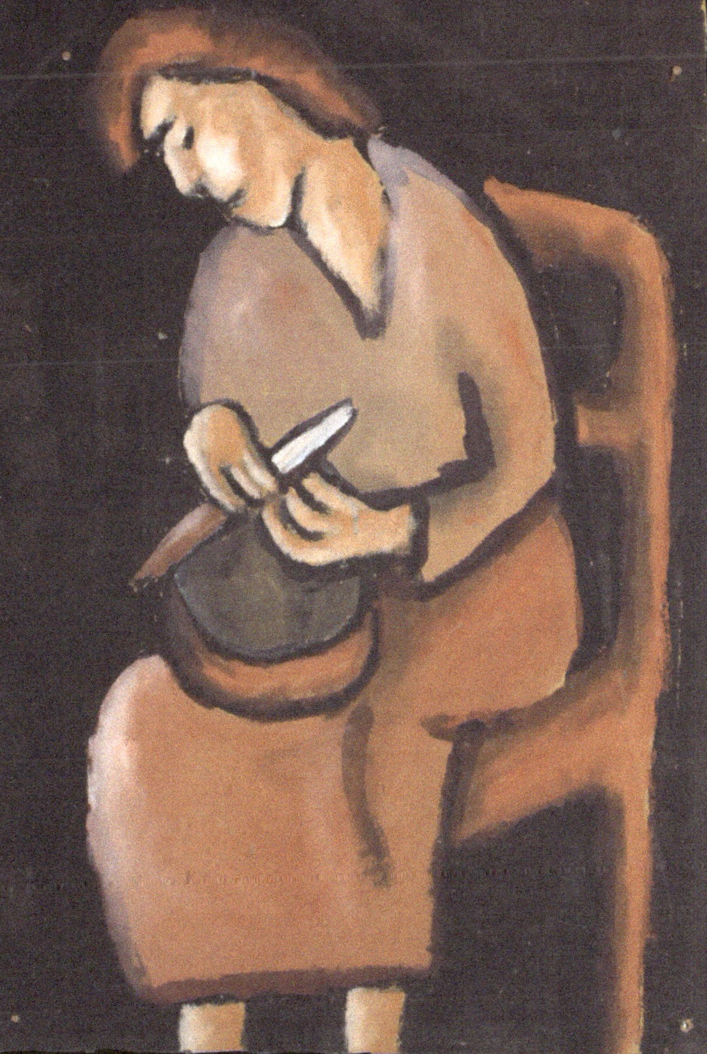
CHARLOTTE WAS PUT TO DO HOUSEWORK

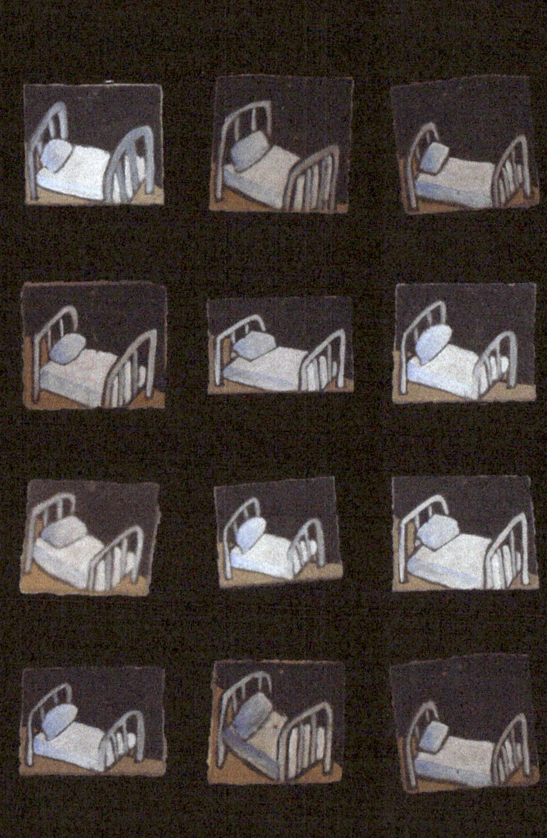

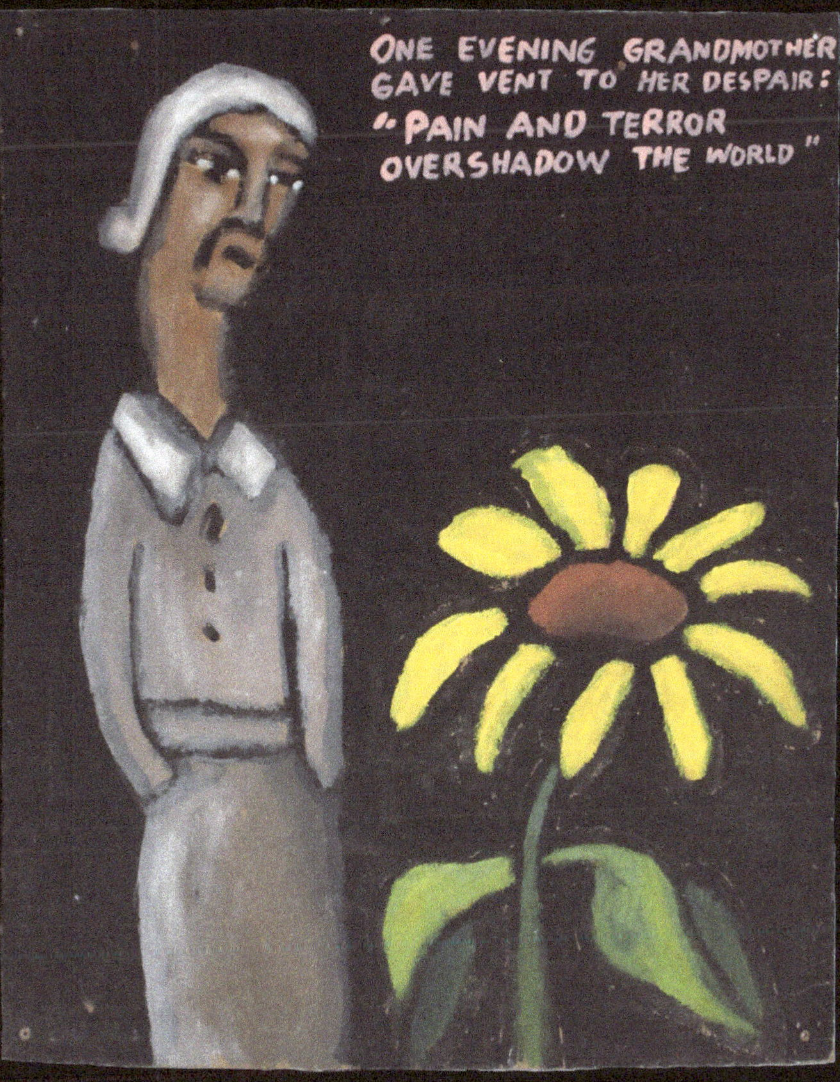
ONE EVENING GRANDMOTHER
GAVE VENT TO HER DESPAIR:
"PAIN AND TERROR
OVERSHADOW THE WORLD"

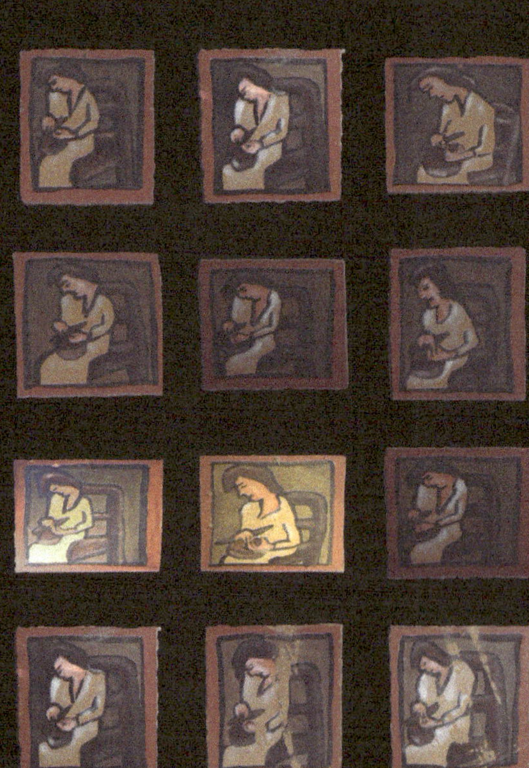

SHE DID NOT WEEP BUT SEEMED LOST
IN AN ABYSS

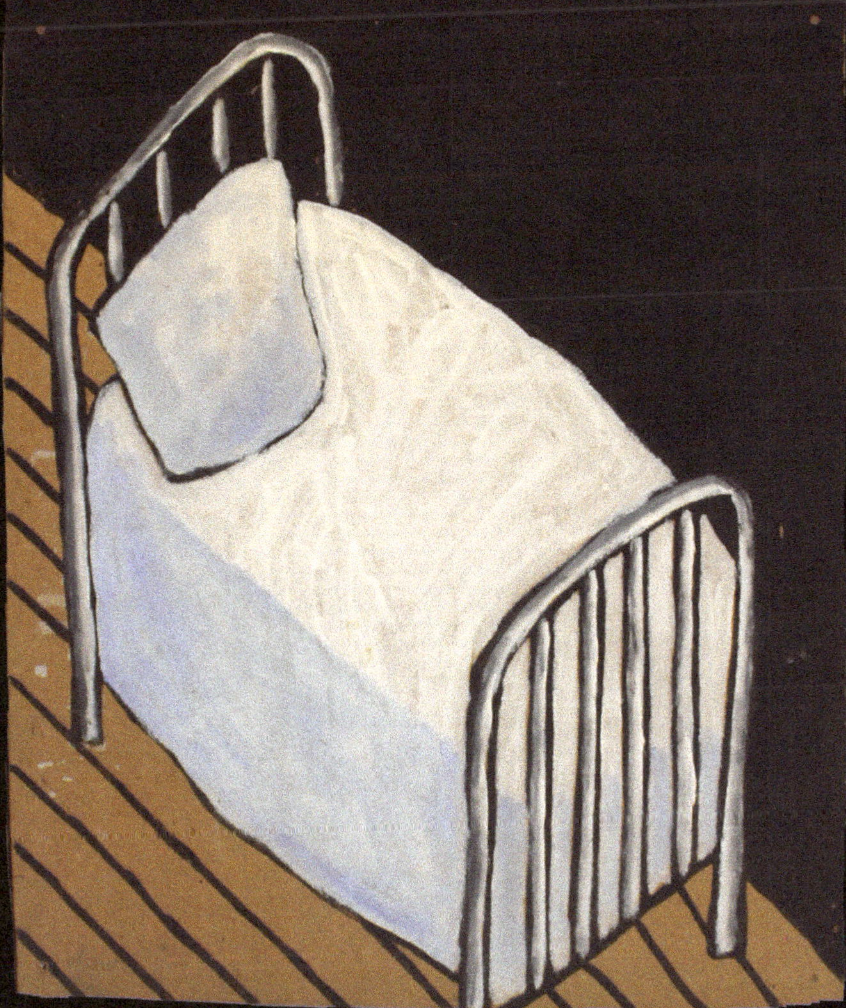

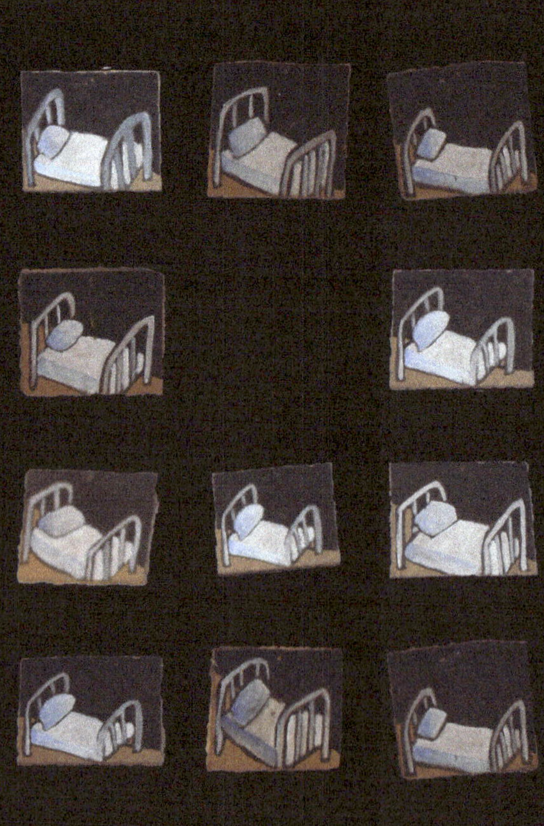

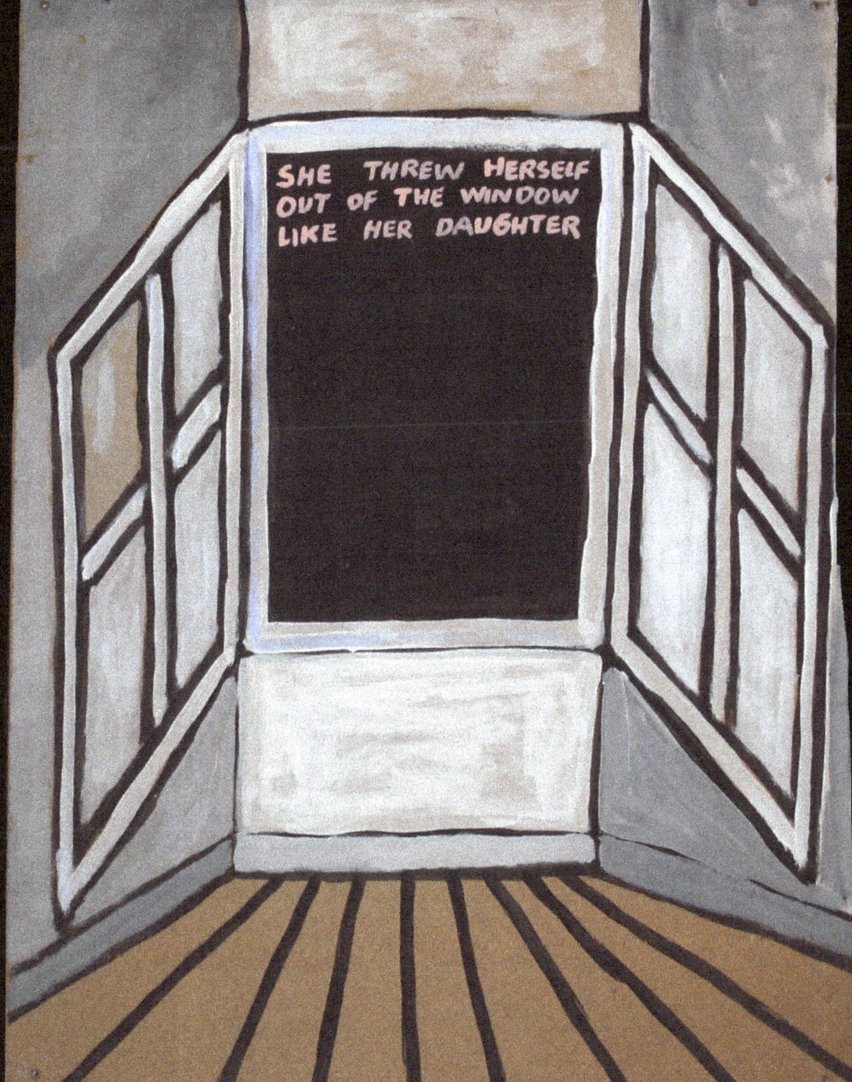
SHE THREW HERSELF
OUT OF THE WINDOW
LIKE HER DAUGHTER

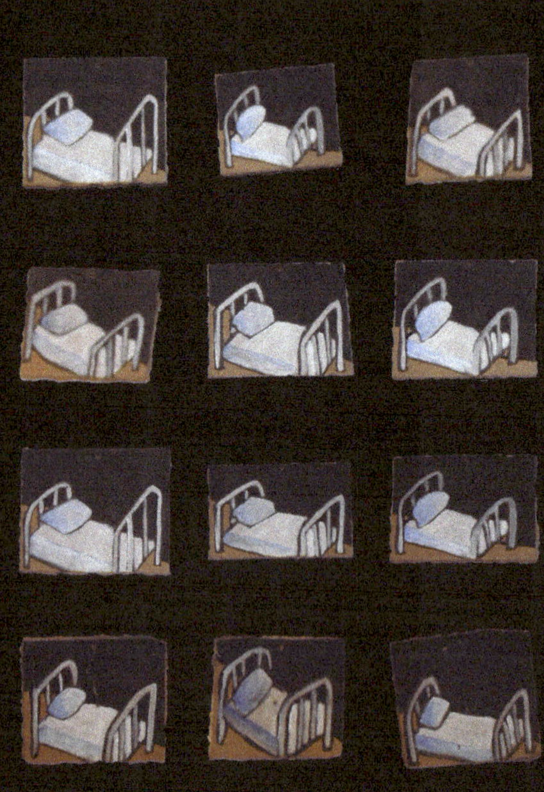

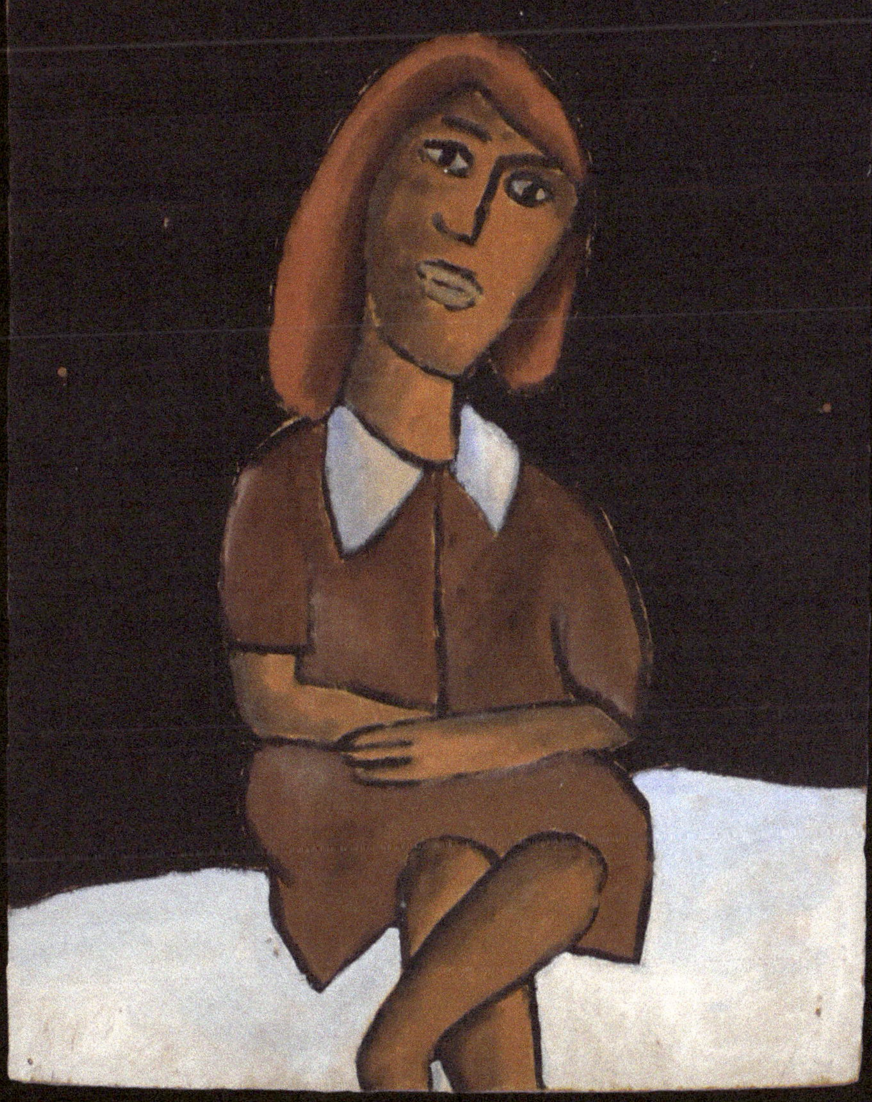
"GRANDFATHER, I FEEL AS THOUGH THE WORLD IS IN PIECES AND NEEDS TO BE PUT TOGETHER AGAIN

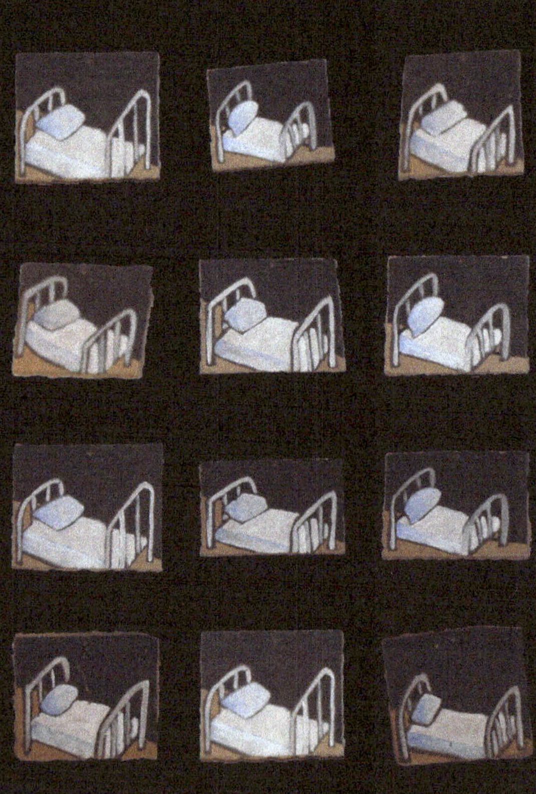

HAD
"I HAVE ENOUGH OF THIS LIFE"

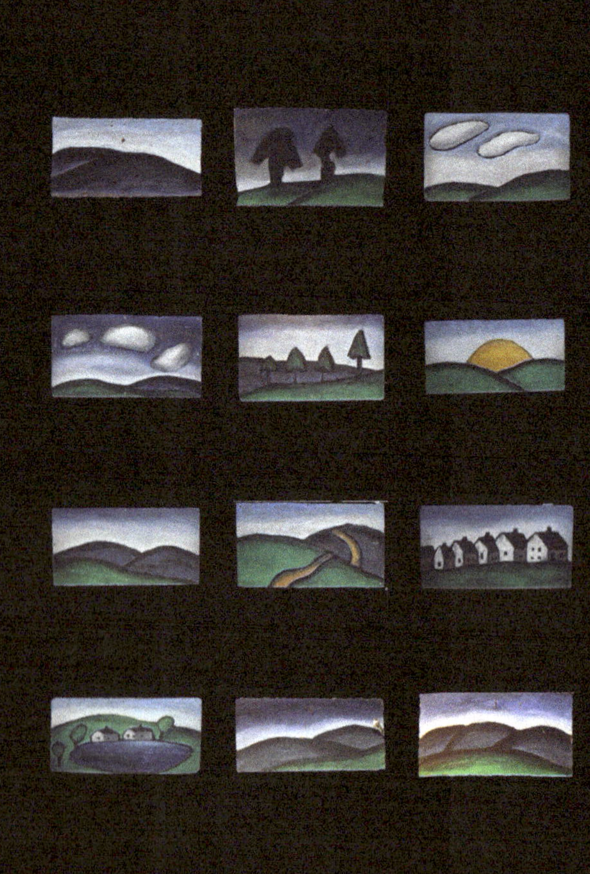

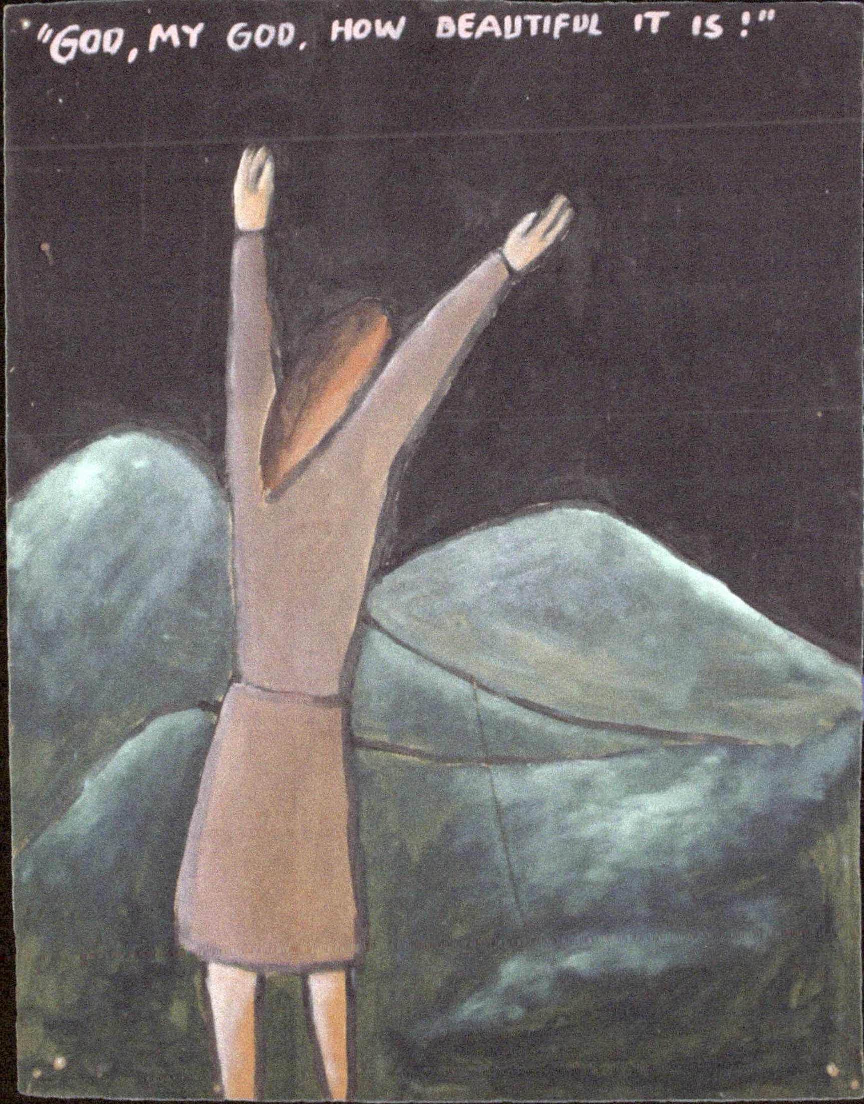

"GOD, MY GOD, HOW BEAUTIFUL IT IS!"

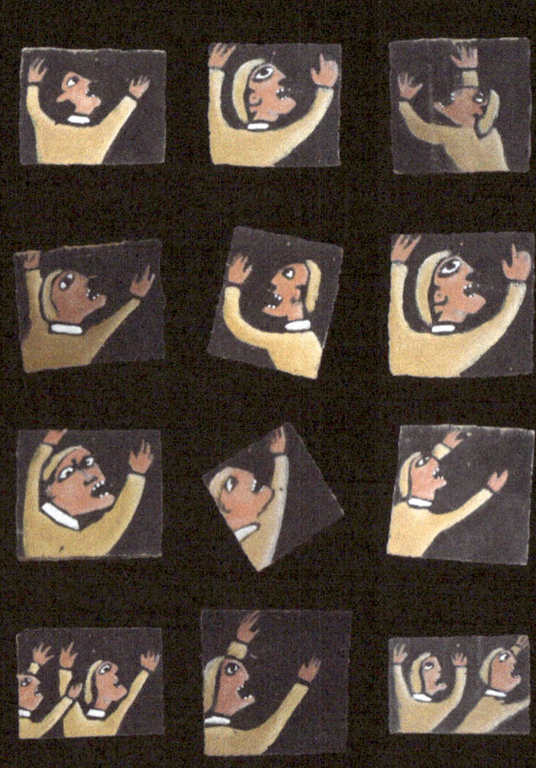

SEPTEMBER 21

1943

A GESTAPO TRUCK DREW UP.

CHARLOTTE WAS DRAGGED OUT OF THE HOUSE AND THROWN INTO THE TRUCK.

SHE DIED IN THE GAS-CHAMBERS OF AUSCHWITZ.

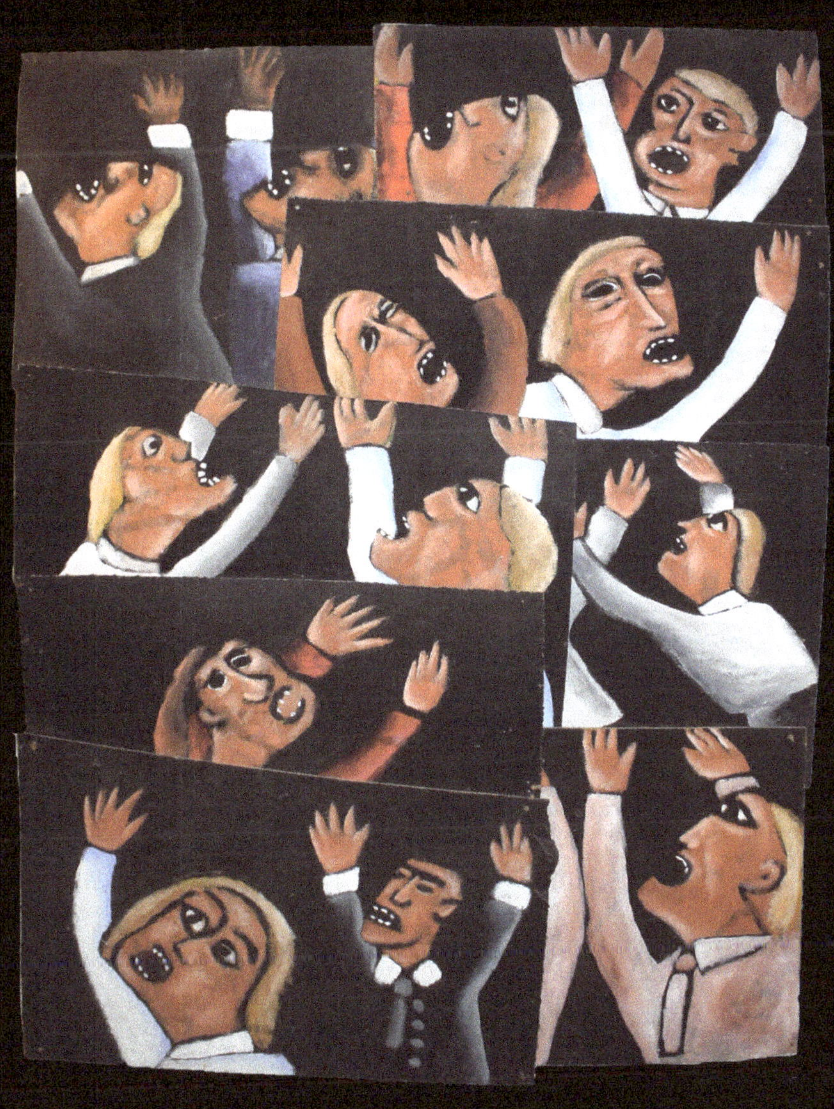

Charlotte Salomon

For me, the only way to see her was to internalize her by painting her paintings all over again, scaling her complex repertory down to cartoon-like simplicity. The moment was right: Margo Sherman gave me a book of her watercolors in the 60's during the reign of Andy Warhol and other populists of the capitalist art market. My own Nazi German childhood with its forever unfinished moral dilemma, transplanted into New York City's Lower East Side slum, all contributed to the intensity with which Charlotte Salomon's work overwhelmed me. German expressionism was my teenage art education: Kollwitz, Beckmann, Kirchner, Grosz, Dix, Modersohn-Becker, Münter all paled by comparison with this truly illuminated book enterprise: the way lettering and writing grow in and out of the images — the rhythmically vibrating pages getting stopped or hurried on by words and sentences more forcefully than in Blake's illuminations.

the lines' brightness or darkness, directions and sizes all splashed over 'the irrelevant microcosm of her life', soaked in so many pains. (2)

That painting's power could stretch into scribbled words and, like graffiti, into public address, I didn't know til I saw her book.

Besides the urgency that ordered me to paint my reaction, I wanted to tell about her, so we strung up the small masonite panels on a wall at theatre for the New City, and Margo Sherman narrated them, cantastoria-style.

In 1982 we mounted them as part of the permanent collection in the Bread & Puppet Museum in Glover, Vermont.

November 4, 2017 Peter Schumann

PETER SCHUMANN is the founder and director of the Bread & Puppet Theater. Born in Silesia, he was a sculptor and dancer in Germany before moving to the United States in 1961.

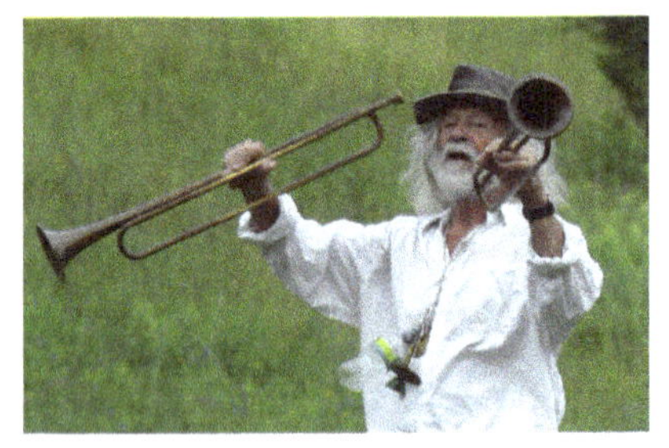

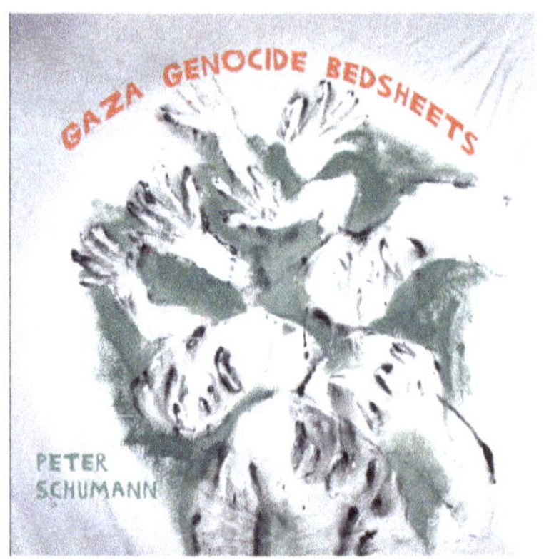

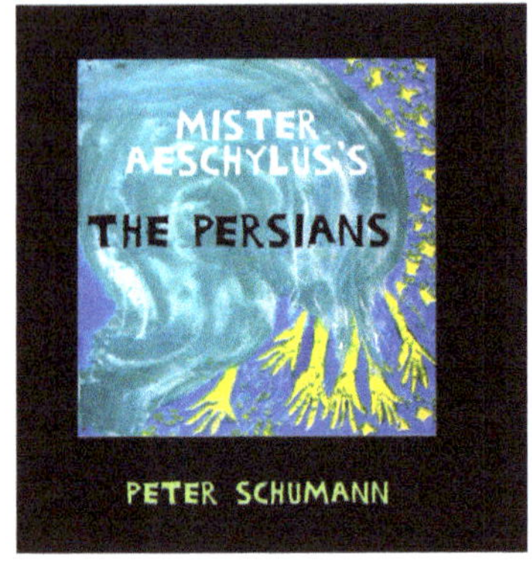

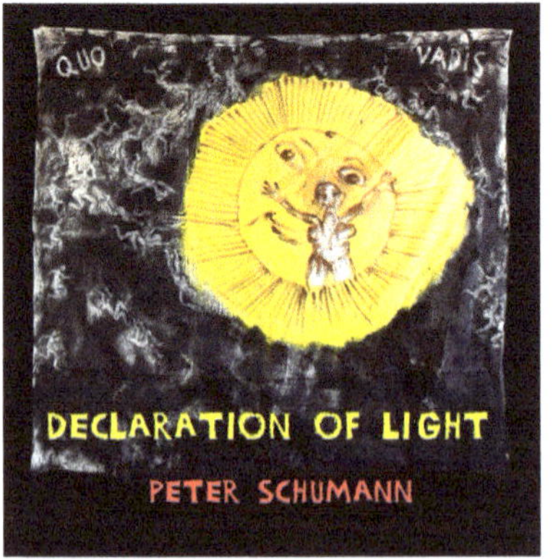

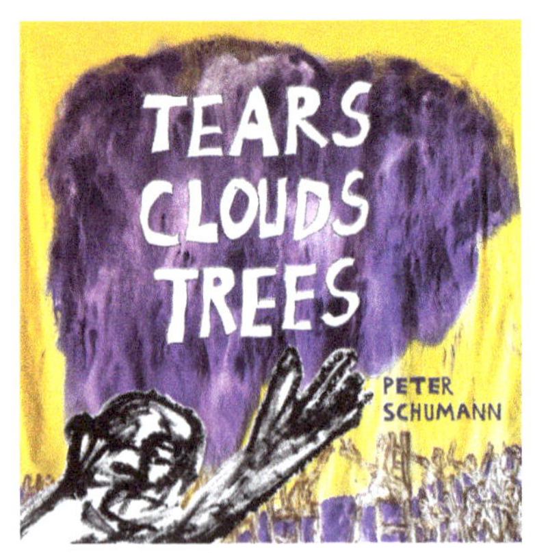

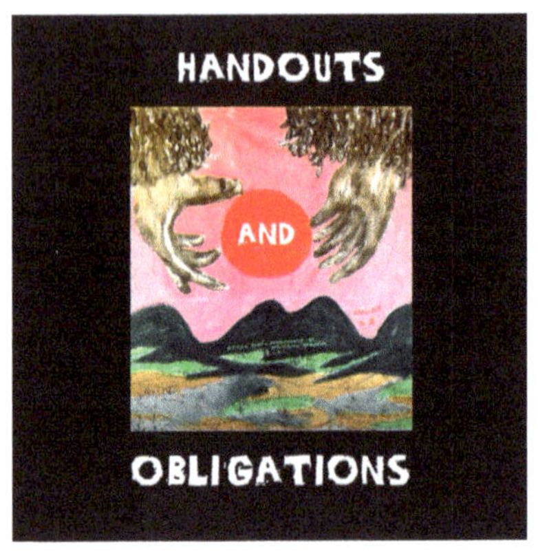

ORDER BOOKS FROM
BREADANDPUPPETPRESS.ORG

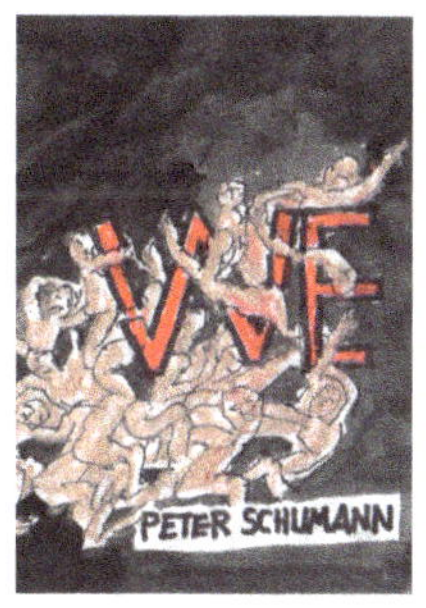

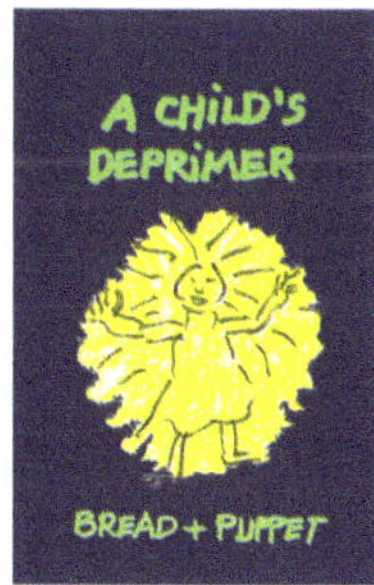

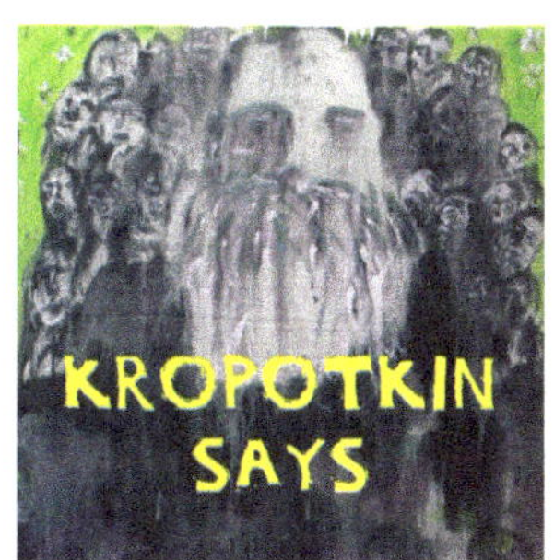

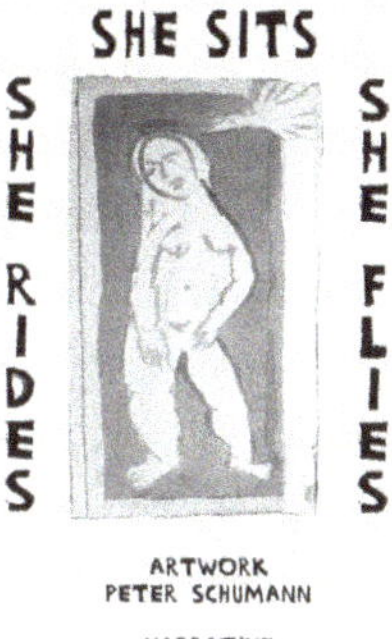

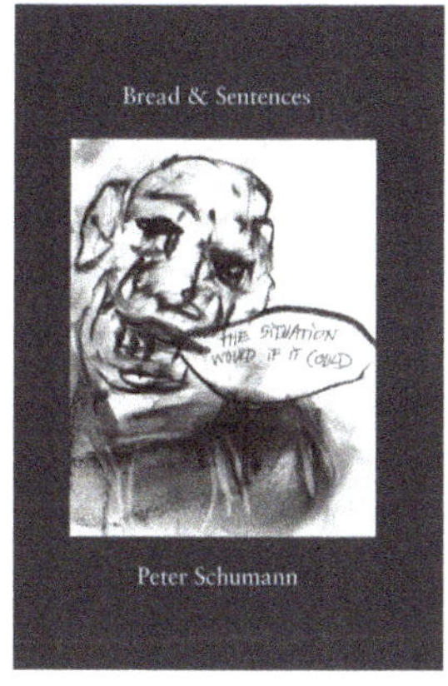

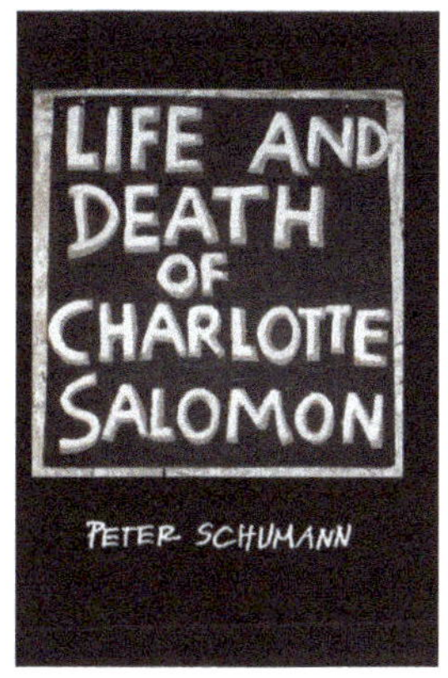

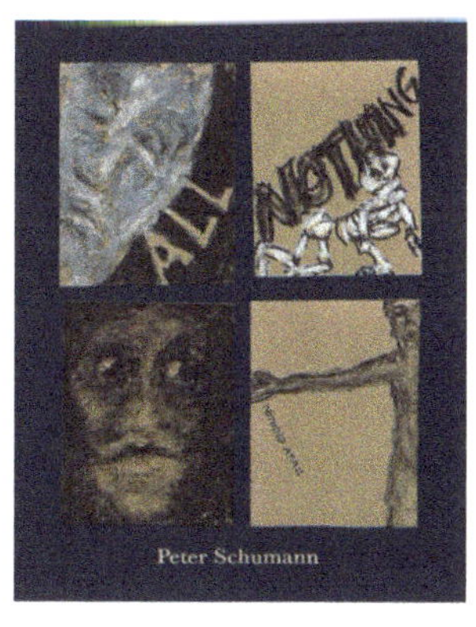

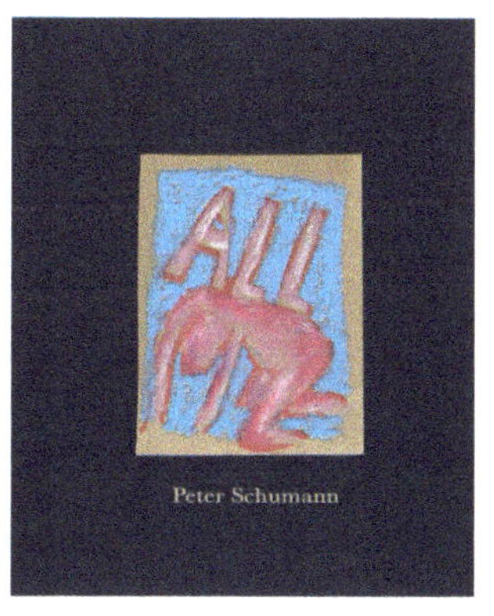

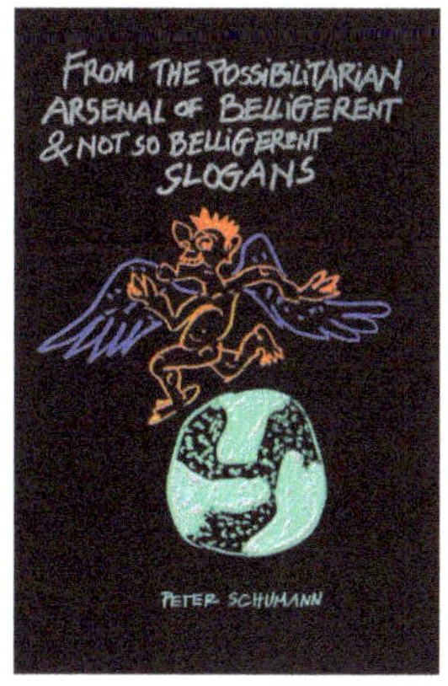

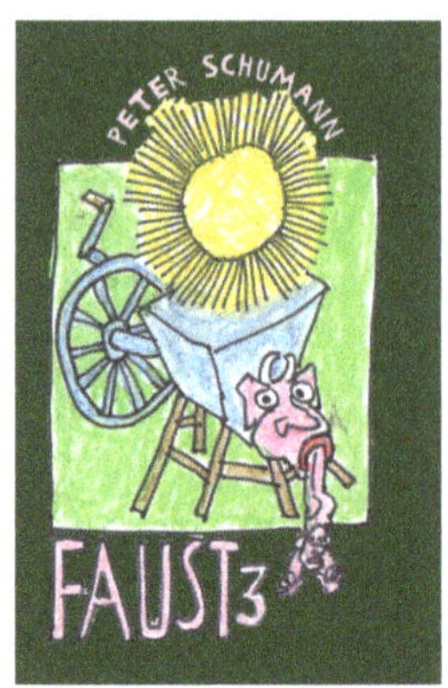
PETER SCHUMANN
FAUST 3

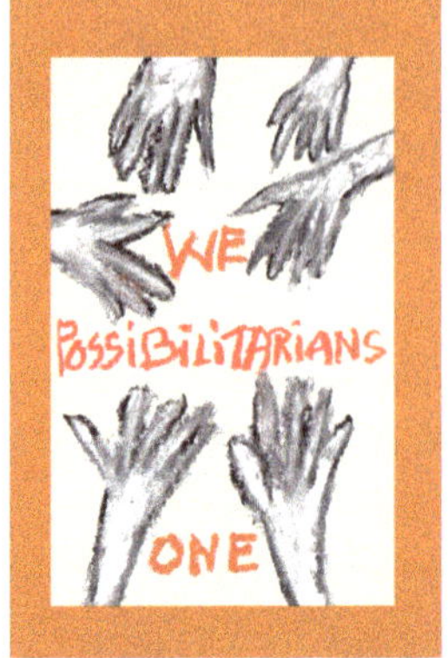
WE
POSSIBILITARIANS
ONE

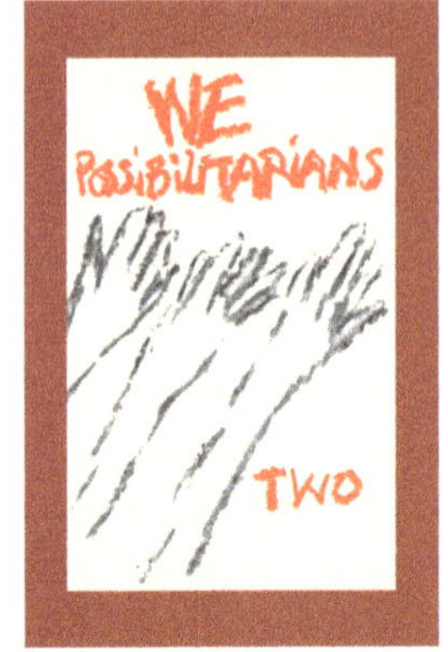
WE
POSSIBILITARIANS
TWO

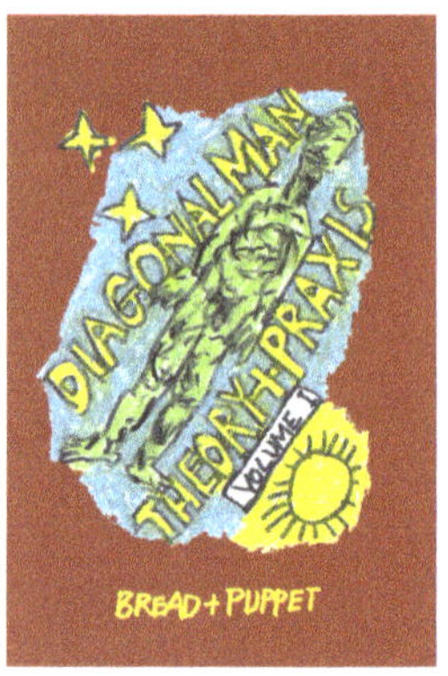
DIAGONAL MAN
THEORY + PRAXIS
VOLUME I
BREAD + PUPPET

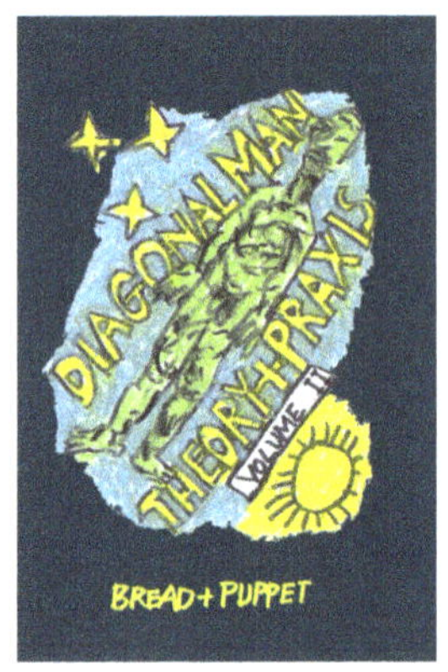
DIAGONAL MAN
THEORY + PRAXIS
VOLUME II
BREAD + PUPPET

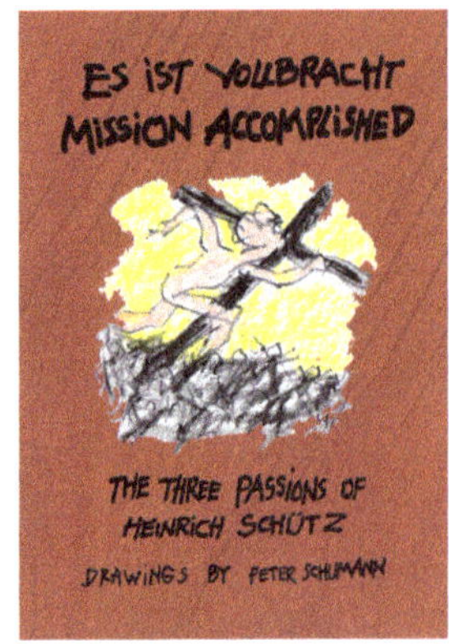
ES IST VOLLBRACHT
MISSION ACCOMPLISHED
THE THREE PASSIONS OF
HEINRICH SCHÜTZ
DRAWINGS BY PETER SCHUMANN

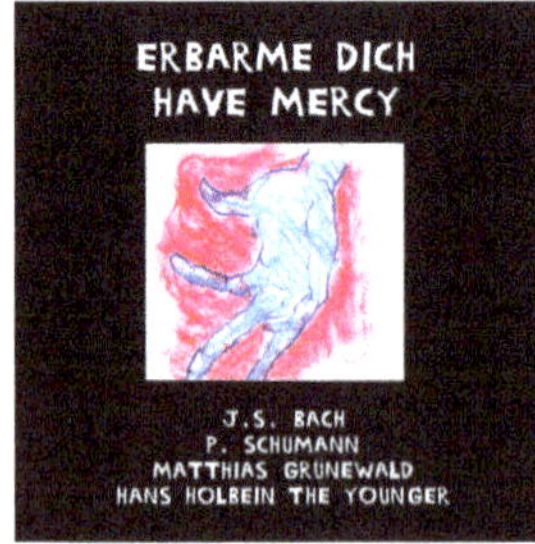
ERBARME DICH
HAVE MERCY
J.S. BACH
P. SCHUMANN
MATTHIAS GRÜNEWALD
HANS HOLBEIN THE YOUNGER

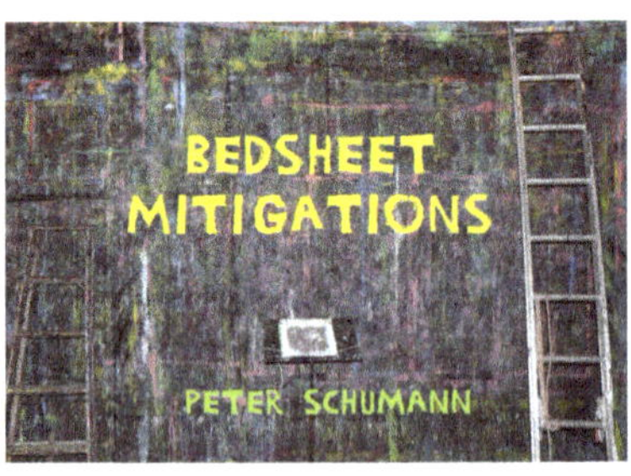
BEDSHEET
MITIGATIONS
PETER SCHUMANN

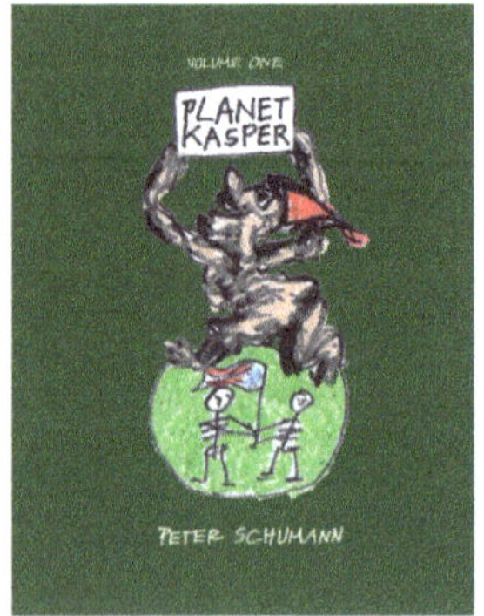
VOLUME ONE
PLANET
KASPER
PETER SCHUMANN

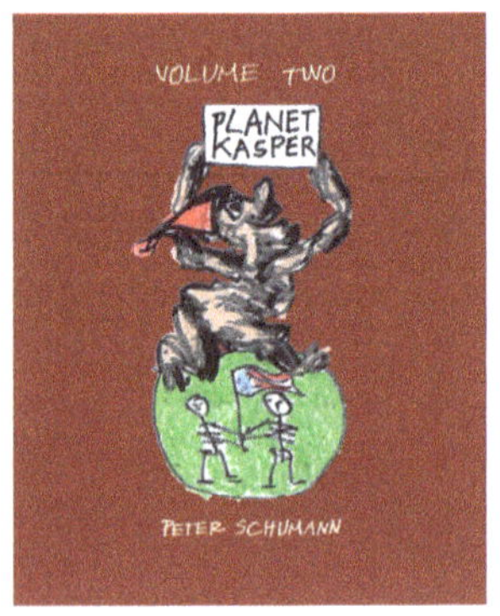
VOLUME TWO
PLANET
KASPER
PETER SCHUMANN

www.ingramcontent.com/pod-product-compliance
Ingram Content Group UK Ltd.
Pitfield, Milton Keynes, MK11 3LW, UK
UKHW062313290726
14090UKWH00018B/1042

9 781944 388324